FINDING GOBI

The True Story Of One
Little Dog's Big Journey

To all dog lovers:
no matter where life takes you,
your dog will always be there for you.

FINDING GOBI

The True Story Of One Little Dog's Big Journey

Dion Leonard

MIX
Paper from
responsible sources
FSC
FSC C007454

FSC is a non-profit international organisation established to promote
the responsible management of the world's forests. Products carrying the
FSC label are independently certified to assure consumers that they come
from forests that are managed to meet the social, economic and

HarperCollins *Children's Books*

Find out more about HarperCollins and the environment at
www.harpercollins.co.uk/green

First published in Great Britain by HarperCollins *Children's Books* 2017
HarperCollins *Children's Books* is a division of HarperCollins*Publishers* Ltd,
HarperCollins Publishers
1 London Bridge Street
London SE1 9GF

The HarperCollins website address is
www.harpercollins.co.uk

3

Text copyright © Dion Leonard 2017

Photographs reproduced by Hermien Webb, reproduced courtesy of KAEM

The author asserts the moral right to be identified as the author of this work.

ISBN: 978–0–00–824452–1

Typeset in Sabon MT and Linger On by
Palimpsest Book Production Ltd, Falkirk, Stirlingshire
Printed and bound by CPI Group (UK) Ltd, Croydon, CR0 4YY

CHAPTER ONE

"Hey, check out the dog!" a man shouted from somewhere in the crowd. "Maybe it's here for the race!"

"Is that right, girl?" another man asked, bending down to scratch her behind the ears. "Are you here to run with us?"

The dog didn't know what to make of all this. There were a lot of people, more than she would have expected out here away from town and right on the edge of the desert. Most of them were dressed funny, but they were nice. Many of the runners stopped to pet her, and more than a few gave her scraps of food.

She was hungry. She was always hungry. She couldn't remember a time when she hadn't been hungry. These people seemed to like her, and when she danced around them they fed her. So she danced. And got fed. And everyone was happy.

1

Then she saw him. He wasn't feeding her. He wasn't laughing or shouting. He wasn't even standing with most of the other people. He was off to the side, shifting back and forth on his big feet. He was tall and skinny, and dressed all in bright yellow. He looked funny, but he wasn't smiling.

The dog didn't know what to make of this tall man. But she decided that she wanted to find out more about him.

* * *

"Well, hello there," Dion Leonard muttered, glancing down at the small bundle of sandy-coloured fur bounding around his feet. "Where did you come from?"

She wasn't a very big dog, he noticed. She was small and compact, and she had big dark eyes and tufts of fur around her mouth that made it look like she had a moustache and beard. He'd seen her with a bunch of the other runners earlier, doing tricks for food. But for some reason she'd singled him out.

It was probably his gear. Dion's running clothes and even his shoes were all bright yellow. He knew he probably looked like a neon light.

He reached down and patted the dog, but he didn't have time to give her too much attention. Today's portion of the race was about to start, and he needed to be ready.

This six-stage ultra race would stretch over seven days and cover almost 155 miles. Dion had never been to China before, but he had done other multi-stage races like this. He used to be good at them. Then he'd hurt his leg. It had been a while since he'd entered a race, and he was worried. This was his last chance, he figured. If he didn't do well in this race, he might as well just quit completely.

He didn't want to quit though. He wanted to compete well – not necessarily to come in first, he wasn't expecting that, but to make it into the top handful, at least. Even placing fourth would be enough to show that he could still do this.

Yesterday had been the first day and he had come in third, so that was an excellent start. But in order to stay in that top handful, he needed to concentrate. And that meant not spending any more time with somebody's dog, no matter how cute she was.

"Better get back to your owner now," he murmured, leaning over to pet her one last time. She looked up at him with those big eyes, almost like she understood him, and barked once. But she didn't go away.

"Take your positions!" one of the race organisers shouted. Everyone tensed and moved to the starting line, completing final stretches. Dion was already done with all of that. He just made sure his shoes were tied tight and his backpack was securely on, and concentrated on the path up ahead. Little pink flags marked the way.

The starting gun sounded, and they were off! Dion didn't try to push past people. This wasn't that kind of race. You had to keep up a good pace, but it was more about endurance than bursts of speed. He knew enough to pace himself. The racers who sprinted out in front now would be worn out later. He had plenty of time.

He concentrated on his footing and his pace but was startled when a small blur appeared by his feet. It was the dog! She hadn't gone away, and now she was running alongside him! Her little legs moved fast, but she was keeping pace.

Despite himself, Dion laughed. "All right," he told her. "If you want to come with me, you can. As long as you can keep up."

The dog barked in response. And kept right on running.

* * *

This is fun! the little dog thought. The bright yellow man was nice after all – he'd pet her and he'd talked to her, and he'd laughed when she started running with him. She liked to run. It was nice to feel the fresh air and watch the ground speeding by beneath her feet. He seemed to like it too. So she settled in and ran with him. They ran together.

* * *

A lot of runners listened to music when they ran. Dion didn't most of the time – he preferred to keep his eyes and ears open. But he did get lost in his thoughts. A part of his brain concentrated on his footing, and the path, and the sun overhead, and the other runners. But a lot of him just tuned out. He thought about his wife Lucja back in Edinburgh, his job, his friends, his family. It helped the time pass quickly.

He wasn't too surprised when he glanced down at one point and didn't see any sign of the dog. She must have got bored or tired or distracted and decided to quit. That was fine. It had been nice having someone to run with, but Dion wasn't here to make friends, even with a dog.

He was here to compete at his best. And now that he didn't have to worry about tripping over the dog, he picked up his pace even more.

Time to get serious about this race.

★ ★ ★

Dion wasn't sure how much time had passed – maybe an hour, maybe two – when he noticed a shadow near his feet again. The dog was back! He hadn't heard her return, but she fell back into step beside him like she'd never been away.

"Welcome back," he told her, and she barked once. She didn't seem to mind the new pace either. For such a little dog, she was fast! And she had stamina too. They'd already been out here for hours, and it was hot, with no shade around for miles. Dion didn't mind, and apparently the dog didn't either. That was fine. "Let's keep moving," he told her, and she just wagged her tail in response.

The dog stayed with him for a while after that. Then the trail led across a small creek. It was about three

6

feet wide, and Dion jumped across without even slowing down. The dog didn't follow though. Her legs were much too short to jump that distance. And the water that ran through the creek was much too fast for her to wade across. Instead she sat down and barked at him, like she was calling for him to stop. Then she whimpered a bit too. She sounded so sad!

Dion didn't stop, though. He couldn't. He had a race to run, and she wasn't even his dog! Instead he just put her out of his mind and concentrated on running.

Dion had only covered a few feet when the barking and whimpering stopped. Then, not ten minutes later, he saw a flash of brown and the dog was back by his side again. *She must have jumped the creek after all*, he thought. *Or somehow gone around.*

Dion laughed. "Determined little thing, aren't you?" he asked. She barked in reply.

When he reached the next checkpoint, people cheered him on. But they cheered the dog even more! "There's that dog again!" they shouted.

The dog wagged her tail and barked happily at the people. They were excited to see her, and she was happy to see them too. Someone gave her some food, and someone else gave her some water.

But she never let the man in yellow out of her sight. There was something about him, something she really liked. He was special.

He sat for a few minutes, talking to some of the other people. But when he rose to his feet and headed out of the tent, she followed. And when he started to run again, she was right beside him.

★ ★ ★

Dion had to admire the little dog. She didn't know when to quit! Well, neither did he. The path led up into the mountains, which was tough. Then back down, which was even tougher because he had to worry more about keeping his balance and not falling. He could feel himself getting tired, but he refused to stop or slow down. One of the other runners, Tommy Chen from Taiwan, was out in front. He was really popular, and everyone figured he'd win. He'd come in first yesterday. Another guy, Julian from Romania, had come in second. Dion had been third. Not bad for the first day and his first race back. But Tommy, Julian, and another runner, Zeng from China, were all ahead of him already. Still, Dion managed to come in a close fourth. He was happy with that. It meant he was still in third place overall.

The dog had been right beside him when he crossed the day's finish line. Even Tommy had noticed. "That dog, man!" he told Dion. "It's been following you all day!"

"Has it had any water?" one of the volunteers asked.

Dion frowned. "I have no idea," he admitted. "Maybe it drank at some of the streams on the way." Someone set out a small bucket of water, and the dog practically attacked it. Dion felt a little bad about that. Still, it wasn't like she was his dog.

When he started to move away, the dog looked up from the water. Then she trotted over to him. And that was that. She followed him to the tent he'd been assigned for the race and went inside with him. He'd brought an inflatable mattress with him – normally he wouldn't have, because you had to carry all of your own gear, but he hadn't wanted to risk hurting his leg again. Now the dog watched as he blew it up, then hopped up onto it as soon as Dion sat down.

Shaking his head, Dion pulled out a packet of nuts and dried meat. You had to carry your own food too. He was about to pop a piece of meat in his mouth when he stopped.

She was watching him intently. But she wasn't

begging. She hadn't whimpered once, other than back at the creek. And as far as he knew, she hadn't eaten anything all day.

"Here you go," he said, tossing the meat in front of her. She wolfed it down and wagged her tail. Then she turned around a few times and settled down. Within seconds she was snoring, fast asleep.

"Great," Dion muttered. "Just what I need, another roommate." He was sharing the tent with several other runners, and three of them had stayed up all last night talking. Now he had the dog to deal with too. And she snored!

But he couldn't bring himself to shoo her away. She'd run hard the whole day, after all. He couldn't blame her for being tired. And if some soft snores were the worst she did all night, well, he could live with that.

Chapter Two

The next morning, Dion smiled down at the little dog prancing around his feet. "You ready?" he asked. She barked in reply.

She'd been curled up beside him when he woke up this morning. "You know what you've got to do now, don't you?" Richard, one of the other runners, asked him.

"What?" Dion replied.

Richard had smiled. "You've got to give her a name."

Dion had groaned at that. She wasn't his dog! But she did seem to have attached herself to him. And he couldn't just keep thinking of her as "dog". Richard was right. She needed a name. But what name?

It should be short, he thought; long names just got shortened anyway. It should be fun and playful but not silly. It should suit her. And it should have something to do with the race, maybe.

Then he had it. Part of this race led through the Gobi Desert. And that was the perfect name for her. Gobi.

★ ★ ★

Gobi was excited. Now she had a name! And the man had given it to her! And he'd fed her and let her curl up beside him to sleep. This was so great!

And now it was daytime again, the sun was out, and it was nice and warm, and they were about to run some more! She couldn't wait!

She was so excited she actually wandered away for a little bit. There were lots of other runners, and many of them said hi to her and petted her. Some even fed her or gave her water. It was really nice.

But once the race got underway, Gobi went looking for one runner in particular. A tall one all in yellow. She found him after a little bit, and he smiled when he saw her.

Then they started running together again.

★ ★ ★

Dion was surprised at how happy he was to see Gobi return. He'd thought she'd got tired of him or found her owner, or something else. But here she was, running alongside him like she'd never left.

Today's race led through a bunch of boulders. The footing was tricky because the rocks shifted around beneath your feet. You had to be careful if you didn't want to get hurt.

Dion slowed a little as he reached the boulders. Gobi didn't. She was light enough that she could leap from rock to rock without a problem.

Julien was the same way. Dion had seen him leap from rock to rock the day before. Today Dion had made sure to be in front before they got to the boulders, because he knew he'd lose some time once they reached that section. Sure enough, he soon heard Julien coming up behind him.

But when Dion got to the top of the pile, he stopped. He could see for miles from up here. There was the next checkpoint, way ahead, just past a small village. There was the starting line, way behind them. There was the path from here to the village – it was nice and flat and straight, and they'd been running on that until the markers had led them up here.

And there was one runner, flying down another path.

It was Tommy.

"Whoa," Julien said from beside Dion. "Not right."

When Dion reached the checkpoint, he stopped and found one of the race organisers. "Tommy somehow skipped that whole rocky section back there. I don't know if he did it deliberately or not, but it's not fair."

The woman raised her eyebrows. "We'll look into it," she said.

Dion still wasn't sure the organizer believed them, but he'd done all he could do. Time to get back in the race.

★ ★ ★

Tommy was way ahead, but the race path curved a bit. At one point, he and Dion were maybe half a mile apart.

Dion assumed Tommy had seen him and would slow down but Tommy continued running fast ahead and didn't stop for Dion so that they could run together as they had before Tommy had gone another way.

Dion tried to catch Tommy. The gap was too big, though. All that happened was that Dion wore himself out, and Julien shot past him.

Dion was mad at himself. He'd had this problem before. He got angry, and then he got careless. During his first ultra race he'd got so angry he'd actually quit the race partway through. He was starting to feel that same way now. Usually his wife was there to help him get over his anger, but she was back in Scotland. Dion was all alone.

Then he glanced down at Gobi, still running beside him. He smiled. No, he wasn't alone. And having that little dog there was enough to take his mind off chasing Tommy down – and everything else. Just having Gobi with him was enough to keep Dion going.

This race wasn't over yet.

CHAPTER THREE

Gobi was happy. The sky was clear, the weather was warm, the ground was firm beneath her feet, and she and the man were running together. From time to time he would look over at her and smile. The warmth of that smile was even brighter than the sun beating down on them, but in a good way. It filled Gobi up.

Then she heard a strange rushing sound up ahead. What was that? Whatever it was, it was getting closer!

* * *

Dion heard it before he saw it. It was the rapid beat of running water. He could tell from the noise that this wasn't another creek. No, this was something a whole lot bigger and faster. Sure enough, as he topped the next rise, he spotted a broad expanse ahead. It was a river! Dion had no idea how deep it was, but the race markers led right across, so he had to assume he'd be able to make it across as well.

With a sigh, he shifted his bag higher on to his back. All of his food was in there – if that got wet, he'd be in real trouble. Fortunately his clothes were made to dry quickly, and he had covers over his shoes that kept out pebbles and things, and also made them reasonably waterproof. That was all he could do.

Drawing a deep breath, he took a careful step into the water. It was surprisingly cold considering how warm the day was, and he sank down up to his waist, but that was it. At least the riverbed seemed solid. He could make his way across, he just had to go slowly. One wrong step and he'd get completely wet. Plus he could hurt himself since he couldn't see where he was putting his feet. This was going to take a while.

* * *

Gobi watched as the man plunged into the water. She wagged her tail, but he didn't look her way. He was clearly busy concentrating. She sat down just beside the water and watched. Surely he would turn around and notice that she wasn't with him. But several minutes passed, and he got further and further away. Finally

Gobi couldn't take it any longer. She began anxiously running up and down the river bank. Was the man going to leave her?

* * *

At the sound of her bark, Dion stopped. He always made a point of facing forward, always forward, during a race. There was no point in looking behind you, after all. It was just about what lay ahead. But this time he did glance back. Gobi was sitting at the river's edge, barking and whining, anxious that Dion was going to leave her. It was the same thing she'd done at the creek the day before. *She made it across that somehow*, Dion told himself. *She can do the same here.*

Except this wasn't the same. The creek had been only a few feet wide, and not much deeper than his ankles. This was at least a hundred feet across and waist-deep on him. There was no way the little dog could cross that on her own, not unless she knew how to swim. And if she could swim, wouldn't she already be doing that?

Not my problem, Dion told himself. He was here for the race. That was it. He hadn't asked for Gobi to follow him. That was on her.

But he'd fed her. And given her water. And named

her. And he had to admit, he liked having her with him. She lifted his spirits.

And right now, listening to her whimper and whine as he left her behind nearly broke his heart.

"Oh, fine!" Dion declared at last. Turning carefully, he started to make his way back. The second she saw him turn around, Gobi was on her feet, tail wagging furiously, her whimpers changing to happy barks.

He was coming back! Gobi was ecstatic! She barked with joy and even pranced in circles as she waited for the man to reach her.

When he was close enough, Dion reached out one long arm and scooped Gobi up off the ground. Then he hugged her to his chest. The little dog lifted her head and licked his cheek, which tickled. Dion laughed.

"Yeah, yeah, you're welcome," he told her. "Now let's get going, okay? Just try not to squirm too much. This is going to be tough as it is."

And it was. Before, Dion had kept his arms out for balance. Now one of them was clutching Gobi instead. That meant he only had one arm free. He had to go even more slowly and more carefully than before. And he still slipped a few times, though never enough to go completely underwater.

Through it all, Gobi was amazingly good. She didn't struggle at all. She didn't bark. She didn't whimper. She just snuggled up against his chest and watched as they slowly inched their way across the river.

Once they'd reached the other side, Dion set her down. She quickly circled him, barking and wagging her tail. Then she nipped at his shoes.

"Yeah, yeah, we're going," he agreed. He was tired from the river crossing, but he knew he couldn't stop now. Especially not with Tommy already so far ahead.

Remembering what Tommy had done earlier was enough to make Dion mad all over again. But this time, instead of frustrating him, that anger gave him strength.

"Let's go," he told Gobi. "Let's see what we can do to cut down his lead."

She barked once, and when he set off she settled in beside him, matching his pace perfectly. Dion shook his head. He didn't know where she'd come from, but this little dog sure could run!

★ ★ ★

The day was winding down, and Dion guessed that the finish line would be visible from the top of the next hill. He and Gobi had kept up a steady pace since the river, and he was pleased with their progress. Once or twice he'd caught a few glimpses of two other runners up ahead. That had to be Tommy and Julien, because no one else had passed him. But the path had twisted enough that Dion hadn't been able to tell how far ahead they were.

Now, as he reached the top of the hill, he looked – and stared. *What?* he thought. There, past a series of small hills, was the finish line, and the tents beyond it. And there were Tommy and Julien, still only halfway there! How was that even possible? Dion had been sure the other two would have finished already.

But they hadn't. In fact, they seemed to be walking. They must have used up too much energy getting across the river.

Which gave him an idea.

"Come on, Gobi," he told her. He hurried down the hill, then raced up the next one. But he slowed just before he reached the top and moved as carefully and quietly as he could. He was tall and thin and dressed all in yellow – if Tommy and Julien looked back, they'd definitely see him. So he sprinted when he was out of sight, and moved quietly when he was visible at the top. And the other two runners didn't look back.

The distance between them started to shrink. Dion ran down each hill and back up as fast as he could, then moved quietly across the top. Gobi somehow understood his intent, because she didn't bark or yip at all. She was as silent as a ghost, though her tail wagged furiously. It was clear she thought this was the best game ever. Together they ran, and Tommy and Julien got closer and closer. But so did the finish line.

Finally, Dion crested the last hill. He was no more than a few hundred feet behind the other two. This time he crept down the hill as well, and together he and Gobi snuck up on the two runners, moving as fast as they dared.

Amazingly, Tommy and Julien didn't look back. Were they that tired? Dion had had a lot of practice running in the heat – he was from Australia originally, so he knew all about hot days. Maybe Tommy and Julien weren't as comfortable in the high temperatures. Whatever the reason, the gap between them kept shrinking. A hundred feet. Eighty feet. Sixty feet. Forty. Twenty.

Dion's foot must have scuffed a rock, or maybe it was his shadow suddenly appearing near them, because Julien finally glanced back and saw him. Dion grinned. Too late!

He put on a burst of speed. Gobi barked and sped up to match him. Together they sprinted past Julien. Then past Tommy.

Dion saw Tommy's eyes widen as they raced by. Tommy struggled to catch up, but staying out in front had worn him out. He just didn't have enough strength left to match Dion's sudden surge forward.

Dion charged past. He crossed the finish line first, with Gobi right beside him. The race volunteers all clapped and cheered. "That was amazing," one of them told him. "You're having a super race!"

Dion smiled and nodded. It was true. He'd come in third the first day and fourth the second, but today he'd come in first. That put him in really good shape. "I owe a lot of it to my little good luck charm here," he said, kneeling down to ruffle Gobi's fur. She barked and licked his face. "Isn't that right, Gobi?"

When he straightened back up, though, Dion was all business. "Can I come by and talk to you later about what happened before the first checkpoint?" he asked the organiser. "I need to clear my head first."

"Sure," she agreed.

★ ★ ★

The organisers did take Dion seriously this time. It helped that other runners also confirmed what had happened. In the end, they adjusted Tommy's time by five minutes. Dion thought it should have been more, but at least it was something.

Besides, he had finished first today. That was something too.

Dion wondered if tomorrow Tommy would go for the win from the start of the race to make up for not winning today.

Gobi didn't seem to mind any of it. She was just happy to eat some of his food, drink some water, and then curl up beside him and go to sleep.

And Dion had to admit, he was getting used to having her there.

CHAPTER FOUR

Gobi was sad. She barked and whimpered, but the man just shook his head. Then he walked away, leaving her with the woman holding her. The woman was nice and friendly, and she kept petting Gobi and giving her treats. But she wasn't the man. Gobi barked again, but the man was already out of sight.

* * *

Dion had to force himself not to look back. It was for her own good, he kept telling himself. Today was going to be long, and hot. Gobi had done amazingly well so far, but there was no way she'd be able to handle the run today. Especially since there wouldn't be any shade or any water. It was better for him to go without her. One of the race volunteers had agreed to keep Gobi safe today while Dion ran. She had also promised to bring the little dog to tonight's campsite with her. But

Dion still couldn't stop hearing the sorrow and desperation in Gobi's voice as she whined and whimpered and barked at him to return.

An hour later, Dion was still gritting his teeth. Only now it wasn't because of Gobi. Something else was frustrating him – or someone else.

Everyone had heard about Dion finishing first yesterday, and he'd got a lot of congratulations from the other runners as they'd lined up that morning. Dion was feeling good, strong, and rested, and he took the lead right away. He had long legs, and they ate up the ground despite the heavy wind. But one runner was deliberately not passing Dion.

Tommy.

Running into the wind was hard. It took a lot of effort, and could easily drain even the strongest runner. But if you were running behind someone else, that person would take the wind instead of you. You'd be able to run more easily as long as you stayed behind the other person. It was called drafting. The polite thing to do would be for two or more runners to take turns – first one ran in front and the others drafted, then they traded places. That way nobody had to fight the wind the whole way. It was more fair if everyone shared in the effort.

Tommy deliberately stayed right behind Dion. Not ten or even five feet behind either. Dion could practically feel Tommy's breath on the back of his neck, that was how close they were. When he looked down, their two shadows were merged into a single long blur.

Which meant that Dion was doing all the work, the whole way. And Tommy was relaxing and drafting, saving his own energy for later.

All through the day, Dion stayed in the lead. And Tommy was right at his heels.

Then, finally, they reached the last of the day's checkpoints. Dion was exhausted. And while he paused to drink some water there, that was when Tommy made his move.

Whoosh! It was like someone had strapped a rocket to Tommy's back. When Dion slowed to a stop at the checkpoint, Tommy zoomed past. Now he was using all that strength he'd saved. And Dion didn't have the energy to stop him.

Julien and Zeng appeared while Dion was still regathering his strength. They nodded at him but didn't pause either. Instead they spotted Tommy up ahead and took off after him. It was clear that Julien and Zeng were hoping to catch or even pass Tommy, just like Dion had yesterday. Maybe they could, although Tommy now had a big lead – and fresh legs.

Dion kept running. What else could he do? But he was frustrated all over again. And he was wondering again if coming here had been a huge mistake. He was tired, so tired, and his legs ached and his head was swimming. Why did he want to keep doing this to himself? Maybe he should just quit. There was no way he could win, anyway.

But he kept running. He could barely feel his legs, and he felt like he was swimming through a fog. But he kept going.

Finally the finish line came into sight. Tommy was long gone. So were Julien and Zeng. Another runner had passed Dion as well. But none of that mattered.

Because sitting there patiently by the finish line was a small brown lump. And as soon as Dion got close, the lump sprang up into the air, unfolding as it went. Now suddenly it was a small, fuzzy brown dog, and it was running for Dion, tail up, tongue out.

And, seeing Gobi, Dion smiled for the first time that day.

It was Gobi's presence, her enthusiasm, and her support that got him across the finish line that night.

Without her there, Dion wasn't sure he'd have made it at all.

Gobi was thrilled to see the man again. He hadn't forgotten her! And he was smiling at her too. Once he'd finished running he scooped her up, and she covered his face in licks. He laughed, and then the two of them crawled into their tent to eat and drink and rest. Gobi had been well looked after that day, but she had still missed him. He was back now, though, and that was all that mattered.

CHAPTER FIVE

Dion glanced around himself. He kept expecting to see a small sandy-brown shape bounding about his feet, but there was nothing there.

It was his own fault. Dion made arrangements for Gobi to travel in one of the race cars again. Today was the longest day of the race, covering over fifty miles and cutting right through a section of the Black Gobi Desert. The temperatures were going to be well over 125 degrees. Tough as she was, there was no way the little dog would be able to handle that kind of heat, especially over that distance. This was for her own safety.

But that didn't stop Dion from missing her.

The starting gun sounded, and they were off. A bunch of runners shoved past, trying to take an early lead. Dion let them. He wasn't too worried. He was having a great race so far, but it was more than that. He was good at the long distances, and at handling the heat. Not everyone was. They were using up a lot of valuable energy by sprinting now, and they wouldn't have a chance to rest and recharge later. Today's race was all about being smart and conserving energy as much as possible.

Fortunately, they didn't have any wind today, and Tommy was off running his own race and Dion didn't see him after the start. Though boiling hot, the day was clear, and Dion settled into a nice, easy stride. He wasn't worried about coming in first. The important thing was to make sure he could cover the full distance. A lot of runners wouldn't be able to do that. As long as he reached the finish line today, he'd be in good shape.

Time passed. Several times Dion saw runners walking, already exhausted. Many of them stared as he jogged by. He just waved, but not meanly. A few even cheered him on, or clapped for him. He waved at them too. He was covering the distance well, and felt good and strong. He had this.

He also decided it was time to finally use his secret weapon – his iPod. The tiny device could only run for a few hours, so he hadn't bothered with it before this.

But on a day like today, it was the perfect way to distract himself and let his body handle the running. Dion pulled out the iPod, put in his earbuds, and hit Play. The music started, and he could feel his spirits lifting. This was exactly what he needed.

Dion did stop at every checkpoint. It was important to refill your water bottles whenever you could, and it helped to check in with the race crew. They were being especially careful today. It was much too easy for a runner to get heatstroke out here. If that wasn't caught in time, it could become heat exhaustion, which was dangerous. When someone had heat exhaustion they got foggy. They could no longer make smart choices – including knowing when it was time to get help. People could die from heat exhaustion, so the organisers were making sure every runner was okay.

Dion felt fine, and the checkpoint volunteers quickly allowed him to keep going. But another runner wasn't having as easy a time.

It was Tommy.

He looked terrible. He was slumped in a chair while several volunteers sprayed him with water or fanned him with a clipboard. But Tommy still looked dazed.

He also looked more tired than Dion had ever seen him. The heat had clearly taken its toll on him and he wasn't looking to leave the tent quickly. Or he was just having a bad day. But Tommy was still one of the people ahead of Dion in the overall race. If he wasn't running well today, that gave Dion a chance to pull ahead.

Dion was listening to his music but still heard the volunteer ask him if Tommy could run with him. Dion agreed because it was what you did, looking after another fellow runner. Races like this were more about doing your best than about beating someone else. And if you did beat them, you did it fair and square. You didn't take advantage of someone. And you never turned your back on a fellow runner in need.

Tommy nodded and rose from his seat. He came over to stand by Dion. He still looked wobbly though.

"Are you sure you're okay, Tommy?" Dion asked.

"Yeah," Tommy replied. "I'm just struggling. It's too hot." His voice was so weak Dion could barely hear him, and he was swaying on his feet. But when Dion started running, Tommy ran with him.

It was even hotter than before. Dion liked that. He enjoyed the heat. He felt good. Only Jax, Brett and Zeng were ahead of him right now, and Dion knew he could catch up with them. This was his chance to take the lead. He picked up his pace.

Tommy kept up, but it was clear he was struggling. Dion felt bad for him, but he didn't slow down.

They reached a long and sandy straight section with no shade. "Come on, Tommy," Dion told the other runner. "Let's run the flags." The pink markers were set in a line every fifty feet.

Tommy sped up to match Dion as they ran to the first marker. Then they slowed down and walked to the next one. They ran the next, then walked, and kept up that pattern for a while. The ground around them became more sandy and rose to form sand canyons. But the track was still straight and solid.

Dion increased his speed again. He was careful not to overdo it, but he was starting to cut into Zeng's lead. He noticed that Tommy wasn't running beside him any more. That was fine though. He must have decided to walk for a bit.

But a part of Dion worried about Tommy. Was he

still okay? He slowed down, and finally stopped. Then he looked back.

Tommy was swaying on his feet, flailing his arms to keep his balance. He looked like he was drunk, or caught in an earthquake.

Dion felt his heart sink. But he didn't hesitate. He turned and ran back towards Tommy instead.

"Tommy, tell me what's going on," he said when he reached the other runner.

"Too hot," Tommy mumbled back. His words were slurred. He pitched forward suddenly, and Dion just barely caught him in time. This was bad.

Dion checked his watch. They were a little more than a mile into this section. The next checkpoint was another three miles ahead. It was just past one, and the sun was right overhead. The day was only going to get hotter. And the only shade around was provided by some rocks maybe half a mile away.

There was no way Tommy would be able to make it back to the last checkpoint on his own. He could barely stand. He had also already drained both of his water bottles. They had only left the last checkpoint thirty minutes ago!

"I need to sit," Tommy declared. He slumped

down in the sand, right there on the path. "Can you wait?"

"There's no sitting here, Tommy," Dion warned him. "You've got to get into some shade." He couldn't carry Tommy back to the last checkpoint. But he did manage to drag the runner towards the rocks he'd spotted. It took twenty minutes, and Dion was exhausted by the time they reached the shade. Still, he didn't have a choice. They couldn't risk waiting for someone else to come along.

"Listen, Tommy," he said once he'd sat the other runner down. "You need help. I'm going to keep going to the next checkpoint and get them to drive back to you, okay?" He knew he could return to the last checkpoint, too, but he just couldn't bear the thought of going backward.

"I don't want to run any more," Tommy mumbled.

Dion nodded. "I know, mate. You don't have to. Just stay here and wait for them to come. Don't move."

Dion had one water bottle left. He handed it to Tommy, then rose to his feet. It was time to go.

★ ★ ★

Helping Tommy had cost Dion a lot. He'd lost forty-five minutes of his time. He'd also given away the last of his water and hauled another man and his gear around in one-hundred-and-twenty-degree heat. That had used up all the energy he'd been saving, and then some.

But Dion couldn't stop now. If he did, Tommy could die. So could he. He had to make it to the next checkpoint.

Half a mile from the checkpoint, Dion spotted a race car. The organisers used them to patrol the race, in case any runner needed help. He flagged it down and told them what had happened.

"You've got to get there quickly," he warned. "He's in real trouble. And I'm out of water myself. You haven't got any, have you?"

The driver handed over a half-empty bottle. They must have handed out all their other water to other runners. It would have to be enough.

Dion made it to the checkpoint and collapsed into a chair. Then he told them about Tommy all over again. He also gulped down as much water as he could. He was feeling weak and queasy. His head hurt and his heart was pounding. But he was still thinking clearly. It was bad, but it wasn't heat exhaustion.

After he'd recovered a little, Dion thought to ask about Zeng. He was surprised to hear that the Chinese runner was only twenty minutes ahead. He must have been having trouble in the heat too.

Which meant that Dion still had a chance to catch up.

But half a mile past the checkpoint, Dion started feeling funny. It was his chest. It felt tight. He was having trouble breathing. When he took a drink, it felt like the water was boiling inside him. He slowed down more and more. Soon he was barely shuffling along.

This was exactly what he'd been afraid of. He was having heart palpitations.

This had happened to Dion a few times before. It felt like his chest was going to explode. He felt sick, and dizzy. The doctors had said he was drinking too much coffee. But Dion had stopped drinking any coffee at all when he began training for this race. So why was he getting palpitations again now? Was it just the heat and the stress and the exhaustion? Or was there something seriously wrong with him?

Up ahead he saw another race car. Dion staggered towards it. They could help him – but only if he could reach them before he collapsed.

CHAPTER SIX

Dion stumbled towards the car. As he got closer, the two men inside jumped out. "Are you okay?" one of them asked. "Do you want some water?"

"I need to sit in the car," Dion replied. "I don't feel very well."

That was an understatement. He felt awful! His head was pounding and his chest hurt and his vision was blurry and he felt like he was about to throw up or fall down or both. But he hoped that sitting in the car's air-conditioning for a few minutes would make him feel better.

It did at first. The cold air felt amazing. Dion just sank down into the seat and closed his eyes. He'd thought he'd never feel cool again!

When he opened his eyes again, he saw the car's dashboard display. "Does that really say one hundred and thirty-two degrees?" he asked.

"Yeah," said the guy behind the wheel. Both he and the other volunteer were watching Dion closely. He knew that if they thought he couldn't continue, they might force him to quit for the day. He couldn't let that happen.

"Can I have the water?" Dion asked instead, pointing at a water bottle sitting in the drink holder. The volunteers nodded, and one of them handed him the bottle. It was so cold some of the water was still ice! Dion drank it down and ate one of his energy gels as well. Then he sat back and waited.

But he wasn't feeling any better. In fact, now that he'd got used to the air-conditioning he realised he was actually feeling worse! His head was spinning and he could barely focus his eyes. The band across his chest was getting tighter and tighter, and each breath was a struggle.

"Come on," he muttered to himself. He knew that he needed to get back outside. Every second he sat here was a second he lost in the race. But somehow he couldn't make himself move. And just thinking about going back out into that heat again made his heart pound even faster. Dion discovered he was panting for air. Then he noticed the volunteers watching him in the mirror. He must have looked like he was dying!

For a second, Dion wondered if he *was* dying. But he refused to believe that. He still had a race to run, and a wife waiting back home, and family and friends – and a small dog he just knew would be sitting there at the finish line, watching for him. He couldn't let her down.

To distract himself, Dion asked about the only runner ahead of him. "How long ago did Zeng come through?"

The driver shrugged. "About twenty minutes before you."

Dion had asked at the last checkpoint and got the same response. So Zeng had only had a twenty-minute lead – until all this. "How did he look?" Dion wanted to know.

The other volunteer shook his head. "Not great," the man admitted. "He was struggling a lot and just walking."

Dion sat up straighter. Walking? If Zeng was walking, he must be out of energy too. Which meant Dion could still catch him and take the lead!

That was all the motivation he needed. With a deep breath, Dion grasped the door handle, shoved the door open, and stumbled out of the car. It was like walking into a wall of heat, and he had to squint against the blinding sunlight. But he managed to straighten up, and then to put one foot back on the path, then the other. He was doing it!

With each stride, his confidence returned and his pace improved. Soon he was running again. Not as fast as he had before, but that was fine. It was enough that he was heading in the right direction, and maintaining a somewhat decent pace.

It didn't last though. After running a few hundred feet, Dion found he had to slow to a walk. He walked to the next flag, then ran from there to the one beyond. Then he walked again. It wasn't the fastest process, but right now it was the best he could manage. Soon he'd forgotten all about trying to catch up to Zeng. Now Dion just wanted to finish the day's run and go collapse in his tent.

Eventually he reached the top of a sand dune and saw the day's finish line up ahead.

And waiting near it in the shade was a certain bundle of sandy-brown fur that sat up and charged him as soon as he was close enough for her to be sure.

Dion smiled as he lurched over the finish line. Gobi

had run the last few hundred feet with him, though after that she ran back to reclaim her spot in the shade. Zeng was already there, as was Brett. They both waved, and Dion waved back. He'd have to find out later if he'd made up any of that time. Right now, though, it was enough to know that he'd completed the day's run. He was still in the race.

Thinking about that made Dion remember where he'd been this afternoon. He spotted a race volunteer and hurried towards him. "Any news on Tommy?" Dion asked.

The volunteer smiled. "It's amazing," he answered. "They got him cooled down and eventually he started running again. Filippo's with him and they're doing okay."

Dion nodded. Filippo was a Swiss runner, and a nice guy. Tommy was in good hands.

For the first few minutes after finishing, Dion just rested. He drank more water too. And petted Gobi, who was thrilled to be reunited with him. Eventually Dion got up and wandered around the camp. Along the way he spotted a clipboard listing the runners' times. He, Brett, Zeng and a woman called Jax were the only ones who'd finished today's run so far. But then he saw Zeng's time and groaned. The Chinese runner had beaten Dion by forty minutes! Dion knew there was no way he'd be able to make that up. There was only one more day of running, and it was a shorter distance than the others – a nice, easy run to finish out the race. Which was great if you were just out to run. But if you were looking to catch up with someone and they were more than half an hour ahead, you probably wouldn't ever catch them – there just wasn't enough time. Which meant he couldn't win the race.

But after allowing himself to be frustrated for a few minutes, Dion took a deep breath. Because, now that he thought about his placement today and what had caused it, he realised something surprising: to help someone in need was more important than any race result.

★ ★ ★

It was another couple of hours before Tommy finally arrived. Filippo Rossi was with him, and though they were both clearly tired, they made it across the finish line together.

People were crowding around Tommy, congratulating him. Everyone had heard about how much trouble he'd had, and the fact that he'd still managed to complete today's leg was nothing short of amazing.

Then Tommy spotted him. Next thing Dion knew, the runner was pushing his way through the crowd. Everyone pulled back to give them a little room – and then Tommy was throwing his arms around Dion and hugging him tight. "Thank you," Tommy said. There were tears in his eyes. "Thank you."

Dion found that he was having a hard time keeping his eyes dry too. So he nodded, acknowledging the thanks. Then he turned away.

The tent felt like an oven, but Dion was too exhausted to care. He inflated his mattress and sank down on to it. With a short bark, Gobi hopped up as well, and turned in a tight little circle before settling down beside him. Dion nodded and petted her head, but his mind was already starting to drift and his eyes to close.

In a moment, Dion was asleep.

★ ★ ★

Dion woke up to hear Mike shouting at him. "Get up!" his friend yelled. Dion blinked. Why did the tent seem so much smaller than usual?

Then his brain kicked in and he understood what

had happened. The tent had been blown down, and judging by the noise howling around outside, they were caught in a sandstorm! Dion grabbed Gobi and crawled outside. The sand stung his hands and face, but he did what Richard instructed and lay down on the tent to keep it from blowing away. Everyone was rushing around and shouting to be heard over the wind. Dion waited for someone to come by and help set their tent back up, but no one did. Finally he and Gobi went looking. They found a woman named Nurali who sent the men around the tents to fix them. They argued about the tent – Nurali said they would fix it, but it could be a while; Dion said they'd already been waiting a while and to make sure everything was taken care of. In the end Nurali just walked away.

The storm continued, and by midnight they heard that it was only going to get worse. The organisers finally decided to abandon the camp for the night. They gathered all the runners together against a row of low cliffs nearby so they could have at least some shelter from the wind and dust and sand. It didn't help much. But Dion and Gobi made the best of it.

Around dawn a bus arrived. It took the runners to

a national park nearby. The park had a small museum by the front entrance, and all of the runners hurried inside. Dion kept Gobi close to him.

* * *

Gobi was having fun. Admittedly, waking up in the middle of a storm hadn't been pleasant, but crawling out of the tent had been an adventure! And then there'd been people running everywhere and shouting. Gobi had barked a few times to join in. She hadn't liked the wind or the sand that got everywhere, but next they'd gone on a bus. She'd never been on a bus before! And it had taken them to this building and put all of them inside. And there were trees in here! Gobi had never heard of trees inside a building before. She could relieve herself without having to go outside! How neat was that?

* * *

Fortunately, the runners were due to rest the day after the longest leg of the race. So the organisers stuck to their schedule and let the runners just relax and take it easy. Many of them bought drinks and snacks at the museum's little shop. Dion spent the time talking with Richard and two of their tentmates, Mike and Allen.

"What are you going to do about that little one?" Mike asked at one point. All of the runners had grown fond of Gobi, but particularly Dion's tentmates. And she seemed to thrive on all the attention. She was certainly enjoying the museum – and the fake trees in some of the exhibits. Dion hoped the museum wouldn't be too upset when they noticed that! Still, their snack bar was making lots of money off the runners, so they shouldn't be too angry.

He considered Mike's question. He'd certainly got attached to the little dog over the last few days. And now he realised that he couldn't imagine leaving her behind. Not even if it meant finding her a good home here in China. Instead, he found himself replying, "You know what, Mike, I've made up my mind. I'm going to find a way to bring her home with me."

Gobi barked and licked his nose. It was almost like she understood – and was saying that she approved.

CHAPTER SEVEN

By the next morning, the storm had passed. The organisers got everyone back on the bus to return to the race site. Today was the last day!

Dion had studied everyone's times while they'd been at the museum. He was still ranked second, but Tommy was no longer in the lead. His trouble during the long stage had bumped him down to fourth place. The other Chinese runner, Zeng, was now in first place. He was the one who'd won the long stage, beating Dion's time by forty minutes. Dion knew there was no catching up to Zeng now, but that was okay. Second was still a really good rank. Third was Brett, the New Zealand runner. He'd been running really well too, and he was the other man who'd beaten Dion at the long stage. But Dion was still ahead of him overall – by twenty minutes. As long as he came in before Brett today, he was guaranteed second place.

Everyone had been exhausted after the long stage. But they'd all had a full day to rest, and today's race was so short there weren't even any checkpoints. So when they lined up at the start, all the runners looked eager and strong. Dion knew a lot of people were going to sprint the whole way if they could. He was planning on setting a brisk pace as well.

Gobi was next to him, as usual. There was no reason she couldn't run this last race with him. Especially since it was cooler today, and overcast. Dion wouldn't have to worry about her overheating.

The gun sounded, and they were off! Dion didn't try to sprint, but he didn't hold back either. Gobi stayed right beside him the whole time, matching his pace perfectly. She was such a good runner!

Several times Dion stopped to give Gobi some water. Each time she drank right from his hand. He was amazed that this scrappy little dog, who had known him less than a week, trusted him that much. And Dion promised himself that he wouldn't let her down.

At one point, midway through the race, Dion was giving Gobi another drink when a runner approached from behind. It was Brett. Dion sighed to himself. If

Brett passed him now, and maintained that lead, Dion would lose the second-place spot!

But instead, Brett stopped beside him. Dion glanced up, and the New Zealander shrugged. "I could hardly run past you as you're giving her a drink, could I?" he said with a smile.

Dion smiled back. "Thanks." This was what the race was like, he thought. Most of the time, the runners respected each other and refused to take unfair advantage of situations. Even though each runner was here to win, they were also all in this together. And running for this long, and pushing yourself this hard, had a way of bringing people together.

When Dion stood up and tucked the water bottle away, Gobi barked and wagged her tail, clearly eager to continue. They began running again, and Brett took up a place just behind them. The three of them stayed like that to the finish line – Dion crossed it fifth for the day, and Brett was sixth, with the little dog right between them. They'd done it! The race was over! And Dion had won second place overall!

★ ★ ★

Gobi pranced about, and the man laughed. She had known there was something special about today – everyone had been so excited and had been running so much faster than before! And it had been so short compared to the other days. Now they were back at camp again, and people were laughing and cheering. So was the tall man. There was lots of food too, and he kept passing her pieces of meat. It was amazing!

★ ★ ★

After the medals and photos came a traditional barbecue. Dion allowed himself to relax and enjoy the evening. The race was over, after all. All his training and discipline had earned him second place – which was really good for someone who'd only been running for a few years, and who had taken a break for the past six months. He'd worried, when he started this race, that his time as a runner was over. Now he knew it definitely wasn't. And everyone else knew that too – coming in second was impressive enough that he'd earned their attention, and their respect. He was happy with that.

He was also happy with the friends he'd made, like Richard and Mike and Zeng, and even Tommy. Every race went the same way for Dion – he started it alone, but ended it surrounded by friends.

And this time he had one special friend. He smiled and ruffled Gobi's fur. She barked and licked his fingers, enjoying the grease from the kebab. Yes, this race had been different for him – because of her. Now he had to make sure that he changed her life in return. For the better, he hoped.

★ ★ ★

After the barbecue, everyone packed back on to buses to go back to the nearest town, Hami. There would be a big awards dinner there that night, and then they would all fly back home.

Except for Gobi.

Because, as much as he wanted to, Dion couldn't simply bring her back to Edinburgh with him. There were all kinds of rules and regulations about transporting animals, especially between different countries. He didn't know what they were, but he knew it wouldn't be quick or easy.

Nurali had taken a shine to Gobi during the race and offered to take the little dog home with her until Dion worked out how to get Gobi home with him.

He'd say goodbye to her now and head home. Once he was back in Edinburgh, Dion could figure out how to get Gobi out there too.

But leaving her behind was a lot tougher than he'd expected. Especially when he saw her glance up and look around. He knew she had to be searching for him.

★ ★ ★

Gobi had been enjoying the morning so far. Everyone was so friendly and relaxed! There was lots of talking and laughing, and plenty of people were offering her food. Especially this one lady. Gobi remembered her from the night of the big storm. She hadn't seemed as friendly then. But she was being nice now!

Then Gobi heard the bus. What was happening? Were they going somewhere again? She suddenly realised that she didn't know where the tall man was. Where had he gone? She looked around and saw that a lot of the runners were getting on to the buses. Had he got on to one too? Why hadn't he waited for her? She started running around, looking for him. But she couldn't see him anywhere!

★ ★ ★

Dion felt like his heart was breaking. He could see Gobi running around outside. Her tail was down and her ears were pinned back. She looked intent and concerned. And he knew exactly why. She was trying to find him. And he was up here, on a bus, about to leave her behind.

He didn't want to go. Not without her. He wanted to run back off the bus and scoop her into his arms and take her with him. But he couldn't. Not yet. So he just sat there and watched. And pretended that his eyes weren't wet and that he wasn't sniffling over a funny little dog he'd only met a few days ago.

★ ★ ★

As the buses pulled away, the nice woman called to Gobi. She offered her some meat and ruffled the fur on her head. Gobi knew the woman was trying to reassure her, but all she could think was that the tall man was gone. He had left her behind.

She lifted her head up and howled.

★ ★ ★

Back in Hami, Dion took a long, hot shower. There hadn't been any chance to do that during the race, and like most of the runners, he hadn't brought extra clothes because they would only slow him down. Now he was happy to strip off the yellow running gear, wash away a week's grime and dirt and sand, and put on clean clothes again. Then he went to the restaurant for the awards dinner. He looked everywhere but didn't see Nurali and Gobi. Finally he asked one of the organisers where they were.

The organiser looked surprised. "Nurali was never going to come here," she answered. "She's got too much to do back at the finish line."

Dion frowned. "Is she coming here at all before we leave tomorrow?" he asked.

The organiser shook her head. "I can't think why she would."

That upset him. It meant he wouldn't get a chance to say goodbye to Gobi after all. He'd always meant to do his best to reassure her that he would be back for her, that his leaving was only temporary. What if she thought he'd abandoned her completely?

And why had Nurali said he'd see them here if she was never planning on coming to Hami at all? Had he just misunderstood her, or had she misunderstood him? That was possible – she spoke some English, but it wasn't her first language, and Dion didn't speak any Chinese. He hoped it had just been an honest error. He was still determined to bring Gobi home.

That night, Dion called his wife. It was the first time they'd spoken since he'd arrived in Urumqi before the race. He was eager to speak to her, and to tell her about Gobi. He wasn't entirely sure how she'd react, though, when he said he wanted to bring the little dog to live with them.

As soon as she picked up, Lucja asked, "How's Gobi?"

Dion was shocked. "You know about Gobi?" he said.

She laughed. He'd always loved her laugh. "Yeah!" she replied. "A lot of the other runners have mentioned her in their blogs, and she's even made it into a few official race updates. She's a pretty little thing, isn't she?"

Dion relaxed a little. "Yes, she is," he agreed. "I wanted to talk to you about something . . ."

But again Lucja was ahead of him. She'd always been good at knowing what he was thinking. "You're bringing her home?" she asked. "As soon as I heard about her I knew you'd want to."

Dion laughed. Leave it to his wife to anticipate his plan. "That's what I'm hoping," he admitted. "But I'm going to need your help." He already knew that she'd agree. That was one of the things he loved about Lucja. She had always supported him. And he could tell that she already liked Gobi, even though the two of them had never met.

The next day Dion took the train from Hami to Urumqi, and then a taxi with Richard from the train station to the airport. He'd fly to Beijing, and from there home to Edinburgh. After a week out in the desert with only the other runners and the race organisers, he'd forgotten just how crowded even a small city like Urumqi could be. It was dizzying, and it didn't help that he couldn't speak the language. But he managed to get to the airport without any real trouble.

On his way to his plane, Dion saw the race organisers also waiting to board. He hurried over to the lead organiser.

"Thank you so much for everything," he told her. "The race was amazing. And thank you for helping arrange for Nurali to look after Gobi until I can figure out how to get her home."

The lead organiser smiled at him. "You're very welcome." Then she handed him her business card. "It's been fantastic to see the story of you and Gobi take shape," she said. "If we can make it happen, we will."

Settling into his seat and waiting for the flight to take off, Dion told himself that everything would work out. He'd get home, fill out whatever paperwork was necessary, and make arrangements to get Gobi brought out to him.

Everything was going to be fine.

CHAPTER EIGHT

"**I**'ve got some bad news."

That was the first thing Lucja said when she greeted Dion at the Edinburgh airport. Not "I missed you" or "I love you" or even "How was your flight?" Those first two he already knew anyway, and could tell just from her welcome-home hug. Instead she got straight to the point.

And Dion knew even before she continued that she was talking about Gobi.

"It's not going to be easy," she explained as they walked towards the exit. "You'd have thought that the hardest part of the whole thing would be getting Gobi *out* of China, but from what I can tell it's getting her *into* Britain that's going to be tough. There's more red tape than you could imagine."

Dion winced. He'd been afraid of this. But he wasn't ready to call it quits yet. And he could tell that his wife felt the same way. "Tell me," he said as they stepped outside and started towards home.

And she did.

The biggest thing was the quarantine. According to British regulations, any animal entering the country had to be held in quarantine for four months before its owners could retrieve it. And to add to the problem, there was only one place in all of Britain where animals could be held.

"Heathrow," Lucja confirmed.

Heathrow was Britain's largest airport, so that made sense. But it was right outside London. And they lived in Edinburgh, up in Scotland! That was four hundred miles away!

"We'll figure it out," Dion declared. They had to. Gobi was counting on them.

But once they got home and started doing more research, they found additional problems. In fact, the more they looked, the more it seemed that China might actually be tougher than Britain after all.

In order to get Gobi out of China, she had to get official blood tests signed by a vet in whatever city she was flying out of. That meant taking her to either Beijing or Shanghai because you couldn't take an animal out of any other city.

But Beijing was eighteen hundred miles from Urumqi. That was thirty-five hours away by car! Which meant Gobi would have to fly from Urumqi to Beijing first. And in order to do that, she had to get approval from a local vet and from someone in the Chinese government.

But there was another hurdle – on the flight to Beijing, Gobi would have to be accompanied by whoever was planning to take her out of the country.

It looked like Dion would have to go back to China after all.

There wasn't much point in going back until everything was settled, though. And that was going to be hard to do from all the way over in Scotland.

"Any chance of Nurali doing all that?" Lucja asked one night.

Dion snorted. "She struggled to help me with my tent in the sandstorm," he replied. "There's no way she'd do all that."

Still, it wouldn't hurt to ask.

They had been looking into using a pet-moving service to make things easier. But most of the services wouldn't help them. It seemed flying pets in and out of China was so much trouble these companies didn't want to bother.

Then they had a stroke of luck. A woman named Kiki said that her company, WorldCare Pet, might be able to help. But they would have to get Nurali to take care of the basic medical work in Urumqi first.

Dion emailed Nurali and was surprised and pleased when she replied right away, especially since she said yes!

"She'll do it," he told Lucja happily. "She says she'll take Gobi to the vet and get all her veterinary tests done. And she's going to buy a crate so Gobi can go on the plane!"

It was great news. Less great was when Kiki told them how much all of this would probably cost.

"Sixty-five hundred dollars!" Dion wailed when he read her email. "And probably another two thousand for quarantine and travelling back and forth to check on her in London." That was almost nine thousand dollars in all! And that was assuming they didn't run into any problems.

It was a lot of money for one little dog. Dion didn't for a second consider stopping, though. Neither did Lucja. In a funny way, Gobi had already become part of their family. And family was more important than money any day of the week.

They did think about how they were going to pay for all this, though. Both of them had decent jobs, but that didn't mean they had nine thousand dollars to throw around. But Dion remembered his conversation with Richard and Mike and the others back in the desert. When he'd said he wanted to bring Gobi home, they had offered to chip in and help cover the costs. Now he mentioned that to Lucja.

"I've got a few emails from them since I got home," he added. "They want to know how it's going with getting Gobi out here, and they've offered again to chip in. I think we should take them up on it."

"I think you're right," Lucja agreed. "But maybe we need to do more than that. Maybe we need to see if anyone else wants to help too." She rested a hand on Dion's shoulder. "Just hearing about you and Gobi from those other runners' blogs made me love her. I bet a lot of other people felt the same way. I think if we tell people what we're doing, and why, we might get more of them wanting to help us pay for all this."

Dion considered that. He wasn't fond of asking anyone for money, or really asking for help in general. But this was important, and it wasn't about him and his pride. It was about Gobi and doing what was best for her. If people wanted to help, who was he to say no?

"Okay," he agreed. "Let's do it."

CHAPTER NINE

"How about this?" Dion asked. He pointed to the computer screen. It showed the crowd-funding page he and Lucja had just created to help pay for bringing Gobi home. Where it asked for their target number, he had filled in "$6,200." "We'd never get it," he pointed out, "but it's probably the most realistic estimate of how much it's all going to get cost to get her here."

His wife nodded. "And if we only get a few hundred dollars, it'll all help," she agreed. "Yeah, let's shoot for it."

Dion clicked the button to finish the site and make it go live. He let out a sigh. "Okay," he said, leaning back in his chair. "It's up. Now we just have to hope that people see it and want to help."

Over the course of the next day, Dion's phone chirped several times. Each chirp let him know that someone else had donated money on the crowd-funding page.

Everyone who had donated so far had been a fellow runner like Richard or Allen. Dion really appreciated their help and their support. He was also touched by the comments each donor left on the page. He hadn't realised just how much Gobi had warmed each of their hearts. That little dog really was something special.

Then Lucja came into his office. She had her phone in her hand. "I've got a guy here for you," she told Dion, holding out the phone. "He says he's a journalist and wants to talk with you about the page."

Dion took the phone carefully. What would a journalist want with him? he wondered. And why would they call Lucja instead of just calling him directly? "Hello?" he said.

"Hi," a man on the other end replied. "I saw your page and had to call."

"How did you even get this number?" Dion asked.

"Oh, sorry, you didn't list a number on the page," the man answered. "But your wife has one on her website." Which was true – Lucja worked as a running coach, so she had her number up on her page so clients could reach her. It made sense, but it was still a little strange.

But the man was still talking. "Listen, I'm with the

Daily Mirror," he said. "I'd like to do an exclusive interview with you about your quest to bring this dog home."

Dion shook his head. The *Daily Mirror*? He knew the paper, of course. Everyone in Britain did. Still, he'd never had a journalist want to write a whole article about him before. And it might at least lead to a few more donations, so what was the harm?

"All right," he said finally. "You want an interview? You've got one."

"Great! But don't forget, this is an exclusive, right?" the reporter reminded him. "No talking to other journalists before the story comes out."

Dion laughed. "Mate, you can do what you like with the story, no one else is going to care about it."

The reporter laughed as well. "We'll see about that," he said.

They did the interview by phone the next day, and the day after that it was in the paper. Dion ran out to buy a copy. He was curious – and a little nervous – about how it had turned out.

He was amazed when he turned to the right section though. The story took up an entire page! And as Dion read the article, he was really pleased. The journalist had done a nice job on it. The title was a little funny – "I Will Not Desert My Ultra-Marathon Pal," it read – but the article really captured the sense of what Dion had said, about how he and Gobi had bonded, and how he felt he needed to bring this dog home because she was already part of his family. There was even a quote from the race's founder: "Gobi really became the race's mascot – she embodied the same fighting spirit as the competitors." It was a good line, and it was completely true. How else could that little dog have run all those miles beside Dion?

An hour later, Dion's phone started going wild. It was chirping almost nonstop. Surprised, he checked the crowd-funding site. People he'd never heard of were making donations! Twenty-five dollars here, twenty-five dollars there, a hundred from someone else. It was amazing!

It had to be the story, Dion thought. He checked the *Daily Mirror's* website. The story was up there as well, and had already been shared and liked by hundreds of people. And it had only been live for a few hours!

Apparently Gobi's story was touching many more hearts than just Dion's, Lucja's, and their fellow runners'. Dion had never expected this, and he was more than a little stunned that it was happening. But he was also extremely grateful.

Twenty-four hours after the story came out, Dion grinned at his wife. "We did it!" he proclaimed. They hugged. They had met their goal! They now had the money they needed to bring Gobi home!

But it didn't stop there. People continued to give money on the site. And Dion started getting calls from other journalists who wanted to talk to him about his and Gobi's story. Then someone from the BBC called. A broadcaster named Phil Williams wanted to interview Dion on his radio show later that night. It was a live broadcast, and Dion was nervous, but there was no way he was going to turn down that opportunity! He did the show, and afterwards the producers created a little one-minute video from his interview and some footage of the race. The video wound up being viewed over fourteen million times on the BBC site!

More radio shows invited him on as a guest. Then he started getting calls from TV shows as well. And not just British shows – a German show contacted Dion, then a Russian one, an Australian one, and several American ones as well. The story had spread worldwide! And so had the donations – people were donating from

India, Venezuela, Thailand – even North Korea. It was absolutely incredible. Dion was almost overwhelmed by all the attention, and this incredible level of support. These people didn't even know him or Gobi! But that didn't seem to matter. They had heard his story, and they wanted to help.

Now that money wasn't going to be a problem, Dion and Lucja turned their attention to the rest of the details. They were happy they could tell Kiki that it was time to move ahead and start the process of bringing Gobi home.

CHAPTER TEN

There was a problem though. In order to proceed, Kiki needed Nurali to take care of the medical tests and paperwork Gobi would need.

And no one had heard from Nurali in several days.

It was frustrating. She was all the way over there in China, and Dion and Lucja were home in Edinburgh on the other side of the world. Dion had tried calling, but no one had answered. He'd sent emails, but those went unanswered too. He didn't even know for certain that Nurali had got any of his messages. And if she had, she hadn't bothered to answer any of them. Which meant they were stuck waiting on her. And that could take a while.

"Nurali's a doer – she gets things done," Dion explained to his wife. "She thrives on being busy and I can't imagine that she's sitting at home with her feet up all the time. She's probably got a hundred other projects going on, and there's no way that she's going to take time off to help us. Looking after a little dog has got to be way down her list of priorities."

Lucja wasn't willing to give up though. "So we need to remind her that this matters," she insisted. "We need her to remember how important this all is, don't we?"

Dion agreed, but that didn't mean Nurali would. All he could do, though, was to keep trying.

* * *

All of the people who had donated to their crowd-funding page were starting to get frustrated too. It had been over a week with no new updates. What was going on?

Dion didn't know what to tell them. He didn't want to admit that they were stuck – at least partially because he didn't want to have to think about that himself. So he just posted that they were still working on it, and that it was going to be a long, slow process. It wasn't enough to satisfy people, but it was all he could do for now.

Kiki offered to call Nurali herself, and Dion happily accepted. Kiki was Chinese, so she could speak to Nurali a lot more easily than Dion could. And maybe

Nurali would be more comfortable talking to Kiki, and thus more inclined to help. It was something, at least.

Dion wasn't going to just sit around and wait though. He called the race organiser who had given him her card.

"This is a big deal now," he told her over the phone. "It's not just me who cares about bringing Gobi back; it's gone global. It feels like there are thousands and thousands of people all watching and wanting to know what's going on. The ones who have donated are like shareholders and they want answers."

The race organiser listened to him. "I'll make it happen," she promised when he was done talking.

Dion nearly collapsed with relief. With the race organiser on his side, Nurali would have to listen.

And she did. A week later, Nurali emailed Kiki. "Everything's fine," Dion reported to Lucja after talking to Kiki. "Nurali said there is a lot more to do than she'd thought, but she's agreed to keep on looking after Gobi for now. Kiki's going to send someone to Urumqi to help make all the arrangements so Gobi can fly back to Beijing."

To make things even better, Nurali sent some

pictures of Gobi. "She's so cute!" Lucja exclaimed upon seeing the images. Dion just nodded. It was tough to see pictures of the little dog and not be able to see her in person. But hopefully that would change soon.

In the meantime, he put the pictures up on the site and posted a progress update as well. That made everyone a lot happier. They'd just wanted to be sure that Dion really was working on getting Gobi back.

A week later, Nurali disappeared again. "What now?" Dion moaned. How many times could this woman vanish on him? They had put up the crowd-funding site two weeks ago, and as far as he knew Gobi hadn't had a single one of those tests yet!

He emailed the race organiser again. This time she didn't reply directly. Instead he got an email from her office.

"She's in America," he told Lucja. "So is Nurali. Her office says she'll talk to Nurali while they're there. That way they can go over everything in person."

Lucja nodded, but she looked a little worried. "Who's watching Gobi?" she asked.

Fortunately, Dion had the answer to that already.

"It looks like Nurali's father-in-law is watching her," he replied. He wasn't happy that Gobi was with someone he didn't even know, but Nurali would be back home in China soon. Then they could finally get this process underway.

* * *

Nurali emailed Kiki once she was back in China, and she promised to get everything moving.

Then she disappeared again.

Dion checked with Kiki, but she said she hadn't heard anything more from Nurali either. He tried the race organiser again but didn't hear back from her at all. And as more time passed, he got more and more nervous.

What was going on here?

Then he got an email from the race organiser. All it said was, "Dion, I need to ring you."

Dion braced himself for the worst as he picked up the phone. "Hello?" he said.

"Hello, Dion," the race organiser replied. And he was sure he heard her sigh. "I have some bad news."

"What kind of bad news?" he asked carefully.

"It's about Gobi." He heard her take a deep breath.

"While Nurali was in the U.S., her father-in-law was taking care of Gobi. Right up until the night that little dog got loose."

Dion forced himself not to start yelling – that wouldn't do any good, anyway.

"How long has she been gone?" he asked instead.

"A few days now," the race organiser told him. "Apparently she did this once before, but that time she came back when she got hungry." The organiser paused. "But she hasn't come back this time."

Dion wanted to scream. Instead he asked the organiser what was being done to find Gobi.

"Nurali's got people out there looking for her," the organiser said. "They're doing their best to find her."

Dion wasn't entirely sure he believed that. Why should any of those people care about this one little dog? It wasn't like any of them had seen the video interviews he'd done or read any of the articles that had come out. China was extremely strict when it came to letting its people access the Internet. Whoever Nurali got to help look for Gobi, it was unlikely they knew that literally thousands of people were waiting to hear that the little dog had been found again and that she would soon be travelling home. Those local searchers would have no reason to care.

Of course, Dion cared. It was just his bad luck – and Gobi's – that he was stuck so far away.

CHAPTER ELEVEN

First Dion told Lucja the news about Gobi. Then he called Kiki. He felt bad for hitting her with such bad news after she had been so willing to help and so nice about all the delays. But he knew it was important to let her know what was happening.

Kiki wasn't upset at him though. Instead she offered to call Nurali herself.

"That would be great," Dion admitted. Kiki had already spoken with Nurali once or twice. Since they both spoke Chinese, Dion hoped she might get more information than if Dion tried.

Kiki called back an hour or so later. She had spoken to Nurali and sounded more concerned than ever. "There's something funny about this whole story," Kiki said. "It just doesn't add up."

Dion agreed. He was upset that Gobi had been able to escape from Nurali's home, and it made him paranoid that Gobi might have gone missing much earlier. Dion had had so much time thinking about Gobi that he had run through every possibility in his head. He was glad to know that Kiki had thought something was strange too.

Still, that wasn't the important part. "What next?" he asked instead. It didn't matter how or why Gobi had run away, as long as she was found again. Before she could get hurt, or worse.

"What we need," Kiki told him, "is to get more people involved in the search."

"How can we do that?" Dion wanted to know. "Nurali's the only person I know in Urumqi."

But Kiki had an answer for that. "I know someone here in Beijing who has experience finding dogs," she revealed. "He runs an adoption shelter. Maybe he can help."

Dion sighed. "Sure, give it a shot. What have we got to lose?" Gobi was already missing, after all – how much worse could it get?

Kiki called back before long. "I spoke to my friend," she started. "He says he's happy to help. And he had some advice on what we should do next."

Dion sat up. Practical advice? Excellent! "Hit me," he said.

"First, we need a poster," Kiki replied. "It has to have recent photos of Gobi, a good description, and the location where she went missing. It also needs a contact number and, most importantly, a reward."

Ah. Dion sat up straighter. This was more like it! At least designing a poster was something he could do. Then his mind caught the last word Kiki had uttered. *Reward*. "How much?" he asked.

"He says five thousand RMB to start with." RMB was the official currency of China, the Chinese Yuan Renminbi.

But five thousand RMB? How much was that really?

Dion pulled up an online currency converter. Five thousand RMB turned out to be roughly seven hundred dollars. He laughed. He'd worried about the reward being some impossible sum, but seven hundred dollars he could live with.

"Anything else?" he asked.

And there was. "We've got to get the poster everywhere, especially digitally," she said. "Do you have WeChat?"

Dion didn't, but he had heard of it. WeChat was like a cross between Facebook and Twitter. But the really big thing about it was that the Chinese government hadn't blocked it.

"Someone needs to set up a WeChat group to start sharing the news," Kiki pointed out. "And then we need people on the street handing out the posters. My friend says that most dogs are found within two to three miles of the place they went missing. That's where we need to concentrate all our efforts."

Two to three miles? Dion shook his head. He and Gobi had run more than seventy miles together in a matter of days! How did they know she hadn't done the same here? She could be anywhere in – or even outside – Urumqi by now! Then again, the race had been out in the open desert. Urumqi was nothing like that. Dion hadn't spent much time in the city but it had certainly seemed really crowded to him. Maybe Kiki's friend was right. He was the expert, after all.

Then Kiki continued, "We know someone in Urumqi. A lady named Lu Xin. My friend helped her with the search when her own dog went missing. He's already spoken to her, and she said she'd be happy to help. She's even willing to head up the search in Urumqi. She's never led a search party before, but she does know the city."

"Wow," Dion managed. "That's amazing, Kiki. Thank you so much." He meant it too. He hadn't known what to do at all. She had given him a place to start and specific things to do, but more importantly, she had found people to help them search for Gobi. The fact that these people half a world away whom Dion had never even met would be willing to help like this was absolutely incredible. Dion knew he was very lucky.

One thing that wasn't so great, though, was the post Dion had to put up the next day. He had put this off as long as he could. All those people who had pledged money had a right to know what was going on. He wrote:

YESTERDAY WE RECEIVED A PHONE CALL THAT GOBI HAS BEEN MISSING IN URUMQI, CHINA, FOR A NUMBER OF DAYS AND SHE HAS STILL NOT BEEN FOUND. WE ARE SIMPLY DEVASTATED AND SHOCKED TO HEAR THAT SHE IS NOW ON THE STREETS OF THE CITY AND THAT OUR PLANS TO GET HER TO THE UK ARE UP IN THE AIR. IT HAS LITERALLY BEEN THE WORST 24 HOURS AND I KNOW THAT MY PAIN AND GRIEF WILL BE SHARED BY YOU ALL. PLEASE UNDERSTAND GOBI WAS WELL

CARED FOR AND LOOKED AFTER IN URUMQI AND THAT THIS HAS JUST BEEN AN UNFORTUNATE INCIDENT.

TODAY THE BELOW INFORMATION AND REWARD HAS BEEN RELEASED ON CHINESE WECHAT. THE URUMQI ANIMAL SHELTER HAS ALSO KINDLY ASSISTED, PROVIDING A GROUP LOOKING FOR GOBI, AND WE ARE ALSO ORGANISING TO EMPLOY LOCALS TO LOOK FOR GOBI ACROSS THE STREETS AND PARKS OF THE CITY.

IF ANYONE CAN PROVIDE ANY INFORMATION AS TO GOBI'S WHEREABOUTS, PLEASE CONTACT US AS SOON AS POSSIBLE. WE HOPE AND PRAY GOBI CAN BE FOUND SAFE SOON, AND WILL KEEP YOU UPDATED WITH ANY PROGRESS.

I'D JUST LIKE TO SAY WE ARE SO APPRECIATIVE OF ALL THE FUNDING AND SUPPORT PROVIDED TO GOBI SO FAR. I CAN CONFIRM THERE ARE STILL 33 DAYS TO GO ON THE CROWD-FUNDING PAGE, AND IF GOBI IS NOT FOUND DURING THIS TIME, THEN NO MONEY WILL BE TAKEN FROM THE PLEDGES.

DION

His phone started to chime almost immediately as people responded. But Dion couldn't bring himself to look just yet. Writing that post had felt like learning about Gobi's disappearance all over again. He wanted to hope for the best, but he knew that the chances were slim.

After all, Kiki had told him that Lu Xin's dog, the one Kiki's friend had helped her search for, had never been found.

CHAPTER TWELVE

Dion tried to concentrate on his work, but couldn't. All he could think about was Gobi. Where was the little dog now? Was she okay? Was she still in Urumqi, or out in the countryside somewhere? Had someone found her and taken her in, or was she on the streets? Was she looking for him?

A lot of people on the crowd-funding site thought so. He had finally read the replies to his post, and all of them were sympathetic. People all over the world said how sorry they were, and how sad it was, and that they hoped Gobi was found soon. Some of them were angry that Gobi had disappeared when she was supposed to be in care in Urumqi. No one was angry at Dion, but he knew that it was still his responsibility. He was the one who had decided to bring Gobi back to Edinburgh.

There were some messages about how they thought

maybe Gobi hadn't actually escaped. That she had been dognapped. Dion remembered his own questions about what had happened, and Kiki's concerns. But there was no way to know about that.

Others, though, thought that Dion needed to go back and look for Gobi himself. They wrote that his bond with her would help him find her – and would let her find him too. And the more Dion thought and worried, the more he started to wonder if that might be true.

Finally he couldn't take it any more. It wasn't that he thought he had magic powers to find Gobi. He wasn't that foolish. And he knew that having locals who knew the area and spoke the language looking for her was better than him stumbling around lost. But as he said to Lucja, "If I don't go and we never find her, I don't think I'll be able to live with myself." He knew it was crazy to think he could find the little dog himself, but he had to try. He had to do everything he could for Gobi. That's what you did for family.

As always, Lucja gave him her full support. "You should go," she agreed. She poked him in the side. "It's not like you're doing any good moping around here," she teased.

Next Dion went to his boss. He was worried about

asking for even more time off. But it turned out that his boss had been following the story as well. "Just go," he told Dion. "Find the dog. Sort it out. Take whatever time you need."

Dion couldn't believe how lucky he was to have people like Lucja and his boss supporting him. He was even more astounded because he and Lucja had decided that they couldn't use the money from the initial crowd-funding for this search. That wasn't why those people had donated. Instead they set up a second site, *Finding Gobi*. Any donations would go towards Dion's trip back to China, but would also help pay for the search party's printing, petrol and food. They set the same goal as before, $6,200 – and they hit it in only two days. It was clear that people still wanted to help, and that they agreed that Dion should go in person.

It made him feel a lot better about the trip. His wife was behind him, his boss had given him time off, and people had donated money to cover his expenses. All Dion was contributing was his time, his effort, and his love.

He hoped it would be enough.

Lu Xin met him at the airport. She was a sweet older lady, but she spoke no English at all. Fortunately, she had brought someone else with her. Lil was a local girl who had been studying English at a university in Shanghai. She had heard about Gobi and had immediately signed up to help.

Dion was relieved to have Lil there to translate. That would make communicating so much easier. But being back in Urumqi still made him uncomfortable. It wasn't just that the city was crowded; it also felt dangerous. Soldiers were everywhere, and so were security cameras. That was because the native Uighur (pronounced "we-goor") sometimes fought with the Han Chinese who had moved here. At times it turned violent. The two groups even set their clocks differently! "Chairman Mao had all the clocks in every region set to the same time as Beijing," Lil explained. "But the Uighur resisted. That was sixty years ago and they still set their clocks two hours behind. When Han Chinese wake up and start work, most Uighur are still asleep." Lil sighed. "We're like two different families living in the same house."

Dion didn't envy her. It had to be stressful knowing that your city had two sides, and both had argued before.

Dion had hoped to go to his hotel and take a quick

nap, at least. He hadn't slept at all on the long flight over. But Lu Xin had other plans.

"She wants you to meet the team," Lil explained. "They spend the afternoons looking in the streets around where Gobi went missing and handing out posters. We'll take you to the hotel later."

He was tired, but Dion knew he couldn't argue with that. These people were giving their own time and energy to help look for a dog none of them had ever met. "All right," he agreed. "Let's do it."

The search team was made up of around twenty people per day but sometimes there were as many as fifty. Almost all of them were women. They ranged from Mae-Lin, a glamorous hairdresser whose own poodle had blue ears and a summer skirt, to a woman Dion nicknamed the Doctor because of her white lab coat. The Doctor smiled all the time and carried dog treats in her coat pocket. She was very nice and very enthusiastic, but she seemed to think every stray dog they saw was Gobi. And there were a lot of stray dogs in Urumqi.

"Stray dogs are a problem in China," Lu Xin explained through Lil. "They roam the streets. We want to look after them. We need to show people that they don't have to be scared."

The problem was that the Uighur thought most dogs were unclean. They would never accept the idea of having a dog for a pet.

But now Dion was confused. Nurali was a Uighur – he had found that out during the race. He just hadn't known what it meant.

"Do you think that Nurali would have looked after Gobi well?" he asked now.

Lu Xin said, "We think Gobi might have gone missing before Nurali thinks she did," she finally answered. "We think Gobi may have escaped earlier."

Dion slumped a little. "How much earlier?"

Lu Xin shrugged. "Maybe one week," Lil translated for her. "Maybe ten days."

Dion wanted to cry. Ten days! Gobi could be anywhere!

But all he could do was keep looking. He had come this far; he wasn't going to give up now.

★ ★ ★

They spent the rest of the day wandering the streets. A few times people called the number on the poster, saying they might have seen Gobi. But each time it wasn't her. One time the dog was even the right type,

Gobi and Dion taking time out -
playing in the desert

Gobi on the Great Wall of China

Missing - Gobi's Chinese reward poster

Keeping warm –
Gobi's first jumper

Gobi on the top
of Arthur's Seat
in Edinburgh

Dion and Gobi's first run
together, back in Edinburgh

a small tan-coloured terrier with black eyes and a bushy tail. But the legs were too long and the tail was too short. More importantly, the dog didn't have any of Gobi's spirit. It kept sniffing at people's legs. Gobi would have been looking into their eyes.

By the time Dion got to his hotel room that night, he was exhausted. He was also depressed. The members of the search team were all wonderful people. It was so incredible that they were willing to give up their time to help him search. But they didn't know Gobi at all. They had only ever seen a few pictures of her. How could he expect them to find her, especially in a city filled with stray dogs? And why had he thought that his being here would make a difference?

Was there any hope at all? Or had this entire trip simply been a giant waste of time?

Chapter Thirteen

The next few days were difficult. Everything just seemed so hopeless. He'd put on a brave face and went back out to search with the team again, but it was just like the day before – they had several false leads, passed out a lot of posters, but got nowhere.

A few good things did happen though.

The first was that Kiki managed to get a local Urumqi TV show to agree to interview Dion about his quest to find Gobi. Dion was happy to do the interview. The article in the *Daily Mirror* back home was what had told the world about Gobi, after all. Maybe this interview could at least let the rest of Urumqi know about the little dog and her plight.

The TV station wanted to know why someone would come all the way from Scotland to look for one particular dog lost in their city. They also liked the fact that locals like Lu Xin were the ones leading the search effort. The interview led to increased local attention. They got a lot of new volunteers, and the search team was now up to fifty people! Some of them even searched through the night, walking the streets while Dion slept. He was immensely grateful that so many people had turned out to help him find Gobi.

Kiki had also suggested that they needed new posters. The old ones had only been printed in Chinese, but the local Uighur spoke a dialect of Arabic. So they ordered new posters with the information in both languages. At least this way no one here could claim they hadn't helped because they couldn't read the posters.

International journalists became interested in Dion and Gobi's story all over again too. It was clearly amazing to them that he would travel so far, but that made it a great human-interest story. Dion spoke with all of them. Every interview or article increased the chances that someone would recognise Gobi, and one good lead was all they'd need.

That was also why Dion let people stop him in the street to take a picture with him. He'd become a minor local celebrity. He had no idea what most of these people were saying, but that didn't matter. They always agreed to take a few posters as well, and Dion figured that had to help at least a little bit.

Dion got to know the other members of the search party a lot better. Mae-Lin was sharp and sassy and always dressed like she was going to a fancy dinner party. Lu Xin was sweet and a little sad – Dion could tell that she was still missing her own dog, even though it had been more than a year. The Doctor was a little odd, but she was also fierce. One time an old man started shouting at them and tearing up their posters by the handful until the Doctor got in his face. She shouted right back, and finally the old man backed down and left them and their posters alone. Plus, she always had treats for any dog they found, and a smile for everyone – except that old man. Their newest member was a young woman named Malan. She had seen Dion on the local TV station. As soon as the interview ended she had called Lu Xin and offered to help search. Malan was the one who picked up Kiki's suggestion and made sure their new posters said the right things in Uighur as well as Chinese. She was also the one to lead them into the more crowded, more rundown Uighur neighbourhoods to distribute those new posters.

The other good thing was that a friend flew out to help with the search. Richard had been one of Dion's tentmates during the race and had been with him when he'd first bonded with Gobi. He had also been one of the first people to contribute to the crowdfunding campaign, even before the *Mirror* article. The fact that he was willing to take the time to come back to China and help meant a lot to Dion. Richard also spoke fluent Chinese, which would be a big help.

Plus, with Richard there, Dion finally had someone to run with. He had started training for the next race as soon as he had got back home but had put that on hold to come look for Gobi. Richard was a good partner for running around the park in Urumqi.

There were a few problems though. When Dion took Richard to meet the rest of the team, Lu Xin looked upset about something. Lil explained that they had got a few unpleasant phone calls.

"Just someone being bad," was all she would say at first.

"Tell me," Dion insisted. "I want to know."

Lil sighed and looked away. "Lu Xin took a call this afternoon," she said finally. "They said that Gobi is going to be killed."

That shocked Dion. It also terrified him. They had already had a few calls asking if the reward would be increased. What if this was part of that? What if someone had Gobi and was holding her until they felt the reward was big enough to bother with? And what if this was their way of saying that he needed to up the reward if he wanted to see Gobi alive again?

Richard helped cheer Dion up. They took the time out to have a nice meal together. They talked about racing, and their homes. Dion found out that Richard had been a U.S. Marine at some point in the past. Richard didn't say why he had left that life behind, just that he had needed a change. But Dion was touched that his friend would tell him even that much. Richard struck him as the kind of man who didn't share a whole lot except with a few really close friends. Richard also admitted that he had more suspicions about Gobi's disappearance – and about Nurali's role in it all.

"None of this adds up," Richard said. "Even without those calls it still looks wrong to me. I don't think it's got anything to do with Nurali being in the U.S. or her father-in-law accidentally letting Gobi escape. I think that the moment Gobi's story went viral and the fundraising kicked in, someone saw a chance to make some money. That's all this is about, Dion. Money. This is a shakedown. The call will come."

Dion didn't want to believe it. Could people really be that awful, to threaten a poor little dog just to make a few thousand dollars? He hoped not. Then again, large parts of Urumqi were poor and rundown. That reward might not seem like a lot to him, but here it was practically a fortune. And lots of people would do all sorts of terrible things if it meant they might gain a fortune.

While they were talking, Dion's phone buzzed. It was a message from Lu Xin.

"Look at this photo," he read. "Gobi?"

The picture was of a small, sandy-brown dog. A deep scar cut across the dog's head. The picture wasn't very clear, but it didn't look like her to Dion. He said so in his reply.

Richard frowned. "Don't you think we should go and have a look?" he asked.

"Mate," Dion replied, "we've had almost thirty of these. They're always the same." He glanced at the address Lu Xin had included. "It'll take an hour and a half to get up there, see the dog, have a chat, and then get back," he explained. "It's getting late and we've got to be up early tomorrow." *For another long day of pointless searching*, he thought. He didn't say that though. There was no point in depressing Richard as well.

Richard took Dion's phone from him and studied the photo. "Looks a bit like Gobi to me," he offered. It was nice having someone else there who actually knew Gobi, but Dion didn't agree. Or at least he didn't think "a bit like" was good enough.

Thirty minutes later, Lu Xin sent another message. This photo was much clearer, and someone had made the eyes bigger and pasted them next to Gobi's photo from the reward poster. Dion frowned and studied the two images. It could be her, he supposed. Maybe.

Richard was more positive. "We've got to go," he insisted. He took the phone and texted Lu Xin to come get them. She replied that she would be right there, and to meet her out front.

Dion wasn't convinced, but he let his friend pay for dinner and then drag him out of the restaurant. At least this time he wouldn't have to endure the disappointment alone, he thought.

CHAPTER FOURTEEN

"**N**ice place," Dion commented as they paused in front of the gates. The neighbourhood they were going to was behind a tall, sturdy-looking wall. They had to wait for the man they were visiting to buzz them in. When the gates finally opened, Lu Xin drove into the compound. All the houses here were large and handsome. They had beautiful lawns and lovely gardens. Expensive cars were parked in the driveways. This was a lot nicer than the other parts of Urumqi Dion had visited so far.

Still, Dion didn't get his hopes up. "We're wasting our time," he told Richard as they got out of the car. Lu Xin led the way up to the house and knocked on the door. A middle-aged man answered. He smiled and stood back to let them enter.

"Maybe," Richard agreed quietly. "But we've got to check, right? You never know." Dion was grateful to have his friend with him. Normally Lucja was the one to reassure him whenever he started to get down. She was still on the other side of the world, but it was almost like she had sent Richard to fill in for her.

Besides, Richard was right. It was possible, and they had to check out every lead. Otherwise they could wind up missing the real Gobi when she did turn up, and that would be their own fault. So Dion followed Lu Xin inside. They headed down a nice wide hallway into a big, fancy living room. It was packed with people, and after a second or two Dion realised that he knew most of them. It looked like the entire search team was here!

Dion glanced around. Lots of people, but no sign of a dog. Was this even the right place? But everyone else was smiling and looked really happy. They wouldn't be that excited if there wasn't a dog around.

"What's everyone doing here?" he asked a research volunteer as he reached her. Richard translated for them.

She laughed. "We all wanted to be here when you and Gobi were reunited," she explained. She waved a hand at the rest of the search team. "No one wanted to miss this!"

"How're you all so sure it's her though?" Dion

continued. "None of you have ever met her." He didn't point out that they had thought they'd found Gobi several times before. The search team hadn't all turned up for each of those dead ends.

But the woman just smiled. "There's something about this one," she told him. "You'll see. We think this is really her."

Dion sighed. "I hope you're right," he replied. "I really do." He didn't want to remind her that they had been sure each of the other times too. It wasn't their fault – the search team members wanted this to happen almost as much as he did. But while there were thousands of stray dogs out there, there was only one Gobi. And he wasn't about to settle for anything less.

He made his way slowly through the crowd. Even though he was taller than anyone else here, he still couldn't see much. Then a group of people stepped away from a long, low couch – and there, sitting beside it, was a bundle of sandy-brown fur.

Dion stopped and stared. "Gobi?" he whispered.

At the sound of his voice, the dog's head shot up. Dark eyes latched on to him. Then the dog shot across the room and jumped up at his knees, tail wagging furiously.

"It's her!" Dion shouted, scooping Gobi into his arms. She started yapping at him, just like she had every time he'd reached the finish line and she was waiting for him. "This is Gobi!" he announced to the room, spinning around. "It's her!"

* * *

Gobi couldn't believe her luck. Ever since the man had left, life had gone downhill. There had been noise and pain and hunger and fear and it had left her head spinning. She had always hoped that the man would come back – she had never even been sure why he had left. Everything had been a blur for so long. Then she had been here in this house with all these people, and suddenly she had heard his voice. At first she thought she was dreaming. But then she had seen him standing there. He wasn't wearing the same clothes or the same shoes, but she was sure it was him. And when he had picked her up, she knew she was right. He was back! He had found her again!

* * *

Everything else in the world seemed to disappear for Dion. All he could see was Gobi. He kept wondering if he was dreaming, but then she would bark or lick his face and he knew he was awake. This was real. He had found her!

Just to be sure though, he stepped away from her to the other side of the room. Then he clicked his tongue the way he always had when he called her. She was at his side in an instant. And when he started to walk away, she matched his stride perfectly.

There was no question about it. It was really her.

She had changed though. And not for the better. Dion headed back over to the couch and lifted Gobi up into his lap so he could study her more carefully. The scar from the picture was even more pronounced in person. It was as wide as his finger and ran from her right eye to back behind her left ear. It was red and raw, so either it had happened recently or it hadn't healed properly yet. Either way, she was lucky to be alive – whatever had caused that scar could have killed her.

Dion wondered if she had been hurt anywhere else. He ran his hands gently over her wriggling body, and she winced when he brushed her right hip. Yes, he'd thought she'd been limping a little as they'd walked just now. She was still using all four legs, but now he could see that she wasn't putting much weight on that paw. Had that happened at the same time as the scar? Or was it from a completely separate incident? Where had she been all this time? What had she had to go through just to get here?

He wished he could ask Gobi herself about what had happened. He was sure she would tell him if she could. But no matter how strong their bond was, she was still a dog. The closest she could get to telling him anything was to bark and yip and occasionally whimper. And to stare him in the eye like she always had. That stare told Dion the most important thing – that Gobi was as happy to see him as he was to see her.

"We're back together, Gobi," he whispered to her, watching her ears perk up as she listened. "And I promise to keep you safe now."

CHAPTER FIFTEEN

The minute Dion announced that it really was Gobi, the room exploded. Everyone had been excited and hopeful before. Now they were ecstatic. Everyone was screaming and shouting and slapping Dion on the back and hugging him and each other. It was very sweet, but it was also a bit overwhelming. Dion could only imagine how Gobi felt at all the chaos around her.

Members of the team kept coming over to take pictures with Dion and Gobi. He let them, of course. It was the least he could do after all their efforts. But when the Doctor came over, she went a step further and picked Gobi up herself. She was a sweet lady and Dion knew she loved dogs, but she must have touched Gobi's bad hip by accident. The little dog let out a squeal – the first time Dion had ever heard her do that – and jumped right out of the Doctor's arms and into Dion's. The Doctor looked crushed.

"Sorry," Dion told her. "She hurt her hip somehow. That's all." He cradled Gobi in one arm and held out the other so that the Doctor could hug him and take a picture with both of them. She was happy with that, and her smile quickly returned. But after that Dion was careful not to let anyone else pick up Gobi. He knew none of them meant any harm, but he wasn't about to risk anything happening to her again.

It took almost an hour for people to calm down enough for Dion to think straight. Then he found Richard in the crowd. "I want to talk to the man who found her," Dion told his friend.

Richard nodded and gestured towards the man who had answered the door for them. "That would be Mr Ma," he explained, leading the way. Their host saw them and waited patiently for them to reach him.

"Thank you so much," Dion said when they were together. He held out his hand, and Mr Ma shook it. "I can't tell you how much this means to me, to have Gobi back again." He waited as Richard translated, and Mr Ma nodded and bowed. "Can you tell me exactly what happened though? I'd like to know the whole story."

Mr Ma nodded and started speaking in Chinese.

He slowed down after a second, smiled, and started again but more slowly. This way Richard could translate more easily.

"My son and I went out for dinner," Mr Ma explained. He pointed to a young man talking to Malan. "My son was telling me about this girl he had seen earlier. That girl there. She was putting up posters. The posters were about a lost dog – your dog. They were written in Chinese and Uighur. But these posters had notes on them too."

Dion glanced at Richard, who shook his head. Neither of them knew what notes Mr Ma meant.

"The notes were handwritten," their host continued. He smiled. "The girl wrote them herself. She was asking people not to throw away the posters. She said it was really sad that your dog was missing, and that you had come all this way just to find her. My son was impressed. He thought that you were very dedicated. And that she was very sweet."

Malan was very sweet. Dion decided that he would have to thank her later. He'd had no idea she was adding her own messages to the posters. But evidently it had worked, at least for Mr Ma's son.

"We finished our dinner," Mr Ma continued, "and

headed home. The restaurant is nearby, so we walked instead of driving. Halfway home, we saw what looked like an old wig by the side of the road. When we got closer, we could see that it was a little dog. She was curled up asleep."

He shook his head. "My son said to me, 'That's the same dog, Dad. I'm sure of it.' I didn't believe him. All dogs look the same to me. But he was certain." He smiled. "He made me wait there so I could make sure the dog didn't leave. Then he ran back to the restaurant. He came back with one of the posters."

Mr Ma fidgeted a little. "I still wasn't sure. They looked similar, yes. But the same? Who knows? My son, though, he was convinced. He called the dog, who followed us home, looking hungry and tired. She's a good girl."

Someone laughed, and Dion glanced up. He hadn't realised that they had an audience. It seemed like the entire room was listening to Mr Ma's story. His son and Malan were standing right behind them, grinning. Mr Ma's son nodded in agreement, and reached down to pet Gobi. She licked his hand.

Their host continued the story. "Once we were home, we gave her some water and food. Then my son called the number on the poster. He also took a picture of the dog and sent it." He laughed. "You said it wasn't her."

Dion remembered how he had dismissed the message. He felt a sharp pang. What if that had been the end of it? He never would have found her – or realised how close he had come!

It was like Mr Ma could read his mind. The homeowner patted Dion on the knee. "My son did not agree. 'It's just a bad picture,' he said. He took another one. Then he scanned in the poster. He sent the two of them together so you could see. This time you agreed."

Except that I didn't, Dion thought. He felt so guilty about that. He still hadn't been convinced. It was Richard who had told Lu Xin to come and get them, and had made him go. If not for his friend, he still would have missed her!

He looked at Richard, who just smiled and shook his head. Dion knew then that his friend would never tell anyone how close they had come to not following up on the photo. It would be up to Dion if he wanted to reveal that. Dion appreciated his friend sticking up for him, but he was big enough to admit his own mistakes. Besides, it had all worked out in the end. They were here, and so was Gobi.

"Well, I can't thank you enough," Dion said finally. Richard translated, and Mr Ma bowed. So did his son. Dion set Gobi down on the couch beside him. Then he rose to his feet and shook hands with both men again. "I think it's time to go back to the hotel," he told Richard and Lu Xin.

"With Gobi?" Lu Xin asked and Richard translated. "You can't. They won't let you."

"What?" Dion stared at them both. "What do you mean?"

Both looked sorry as Richard translated again, "No hotel in the city would ever let you bring a dog inside. It just isn't done. Too many people around here feel that dogs are unclean, remember? If they thought a hotel was letting dogs in, no one would ever go there again. It's too big a risk."

Dion frowned. "Really?" he asked. He had forgotten about the local attitude towards dogs. He was so used to the search team, who all loved dogs! "But after all this?" he continued. He looked down at Gobi. She had sniffed the couch, turned around, and then plopped down to sleep. Just like she had done back in their tent during the race. "After all she's been through?"

Richard shook his head. "They're right," he confirmed. "Maybe you can try and talk to the manager and see if he'll let you, but I doubt it. I stay in hotels all over China and I've never seen a dog in one."

Dion checked his watch. It was after eleven at night. How had it got so late? Suddenly he was exhausted. It had been a very busy and very emotional day.

Lu Xin rested a hand on his shoulder. "We should ask Mr Ma to keep her here tonight," she suggested gently. "Then you can buy all the things you need for her, like a lead and collar, food, bowls, and a bed, and collect her tomorrow."

Dion sighed. He knew she was probably right. He had no idea what to do now that he had actually found Gobi – he had never thought this far ahead. He would have to talk to Kiki and start the process of bringing Gobi home. But between here and there he had no idea.

He turned to Mr Ma. "I'm sorry to ask this after everything you've already done," he said, then waited as Richard translated. "But would you be willing to let her stay here for tonight? I need to make arrangements. I can come back and collect her tomorrow."

Mr Ma bowed. "It would be our pleasure," he replied. His son nodded as well. That made Dion feel a little better. At least he knew Gobi would be somewhere safe tonight.

He turned to Gobi again. She was sound asleep and snoring softly. Every so often a paw would twitch, just like it had at night during the race. Dion had always thought she was dreaming about running. Maybe even about running with him.

Dion knelt down and ruffled her fur gently, careful not to wake her. "I'm sorry, girl," he said softly. "I've got a lot to learn about being your dad, haven't I?" Her ear twitched in response but she stayed asleep.

It was hard to leave Gobi there, and Dion kept turning around to glance back at her on the couch. A part of him felt like if he let her out of his sight now, he would never see her again. But he told himself he was being silly. She was safe now. The Mas would take good care of her tonight. And he would be back to get her tomorrow. That was all, just one night.

Richard still had to practically push him out the door and into the car.

Dion barely remembered the ride back to the hotel, or stumbling inside and upstairs into his room. As soon as he was there, though, he called Lucja. "We bloody well found her!" he yelled the second she picked up. She let out a shout of pure joy. Dion could tell from the sound that she was crying. That was okay. So was he.

CHAPTER SIXTEEN

The next morning, Dion felt better than he had for a while. He had found Gobi, and he had finally got some sleep. Things were definitely looking up.

He and Richard met up for breakfast. Then they went shopping. They managed to find a store with a pet selection and bought Gobi a leash and collar and some bowls and some dog food. That would have to do for now.

Dion also spoke to Kiki. She was thrilled that he had found Gobi and happy to know that she could finally start helping him get the little dog to Edinburgh. Not that it was going to be easy.

"We need to get her to a vet," Kiki told him. "Nurali didn't take care of any of that, so now we have to do it. Gobi will have to have her medical certificate before we can get approval for her to fly."

"How long will that take?" Dion asked.

"Maybe a week, maybe a month," Kiki replied. "It depends how long we have to wait to see the vet."

Dion felt a little of his good mood slip away. A week or a month? Or more? "Are you sure we have to fly?" he tried. "Why don't we drive?"

Kiki laughed. "It's a thirty-hour drive and no hotel will let you take her inside with you," she reminded him. "Would you really want to leave her in the car?"

No, Dion did not want to do that. It wasn't even remotely safe.

"Besides," Kiki added, "I have a contact at an airline who says she might be able to get Gobi on a flight earlier than we think."

"That would be great," Dion agreed. But he still had to figure out what he and Gobi were going to do for the next week or month until they could see the vet.

First, though, he had to figure out what to do with her tonight.

After talking with Kiki, Dion went down to the lobby to speak with the hotel manager about letting Gobi stay in the room with him.

"No," the manager said.

Dion tried again. Maybe the manager hadn't understood him. After all, the man had been very helpful during the search. He had even let them use a meeting room for interviews. "Can the dog stay in my room?" Dion repeated now. "She's only little." He held up his hands to show Gobi's approximate size. "It'll be good publicity for you," he added. That was the real winner, he knew. The interview had already been all over television, local and national. And it had shown the name of the hotel too. Surely if Dion was able to post that he and Gobi were safe here, that would drum up even more business for them?

But the manager still shook his head. "No," he repeated. "We don't ever let dogs stay in the hotel." Then he paused. "But I would be willing to help," he said very softly.

Great, Dion thought. The man wanted to be paid for helping. Well, it was worth it.

But then the manager continued. "So perhaps the dog could stay in one of the rooms we use for staff training."

Hm. That wasn't what Dion had expected, but still it was something. And if the training room was anything like the hotel's meeting rooms, that would be just fine. "Can I see it?" he asked.

"Of course." The manager came out from behind

the big front desk. Dion expected the man to lead him upstairs or down the hall, but instead he turned towards the front door. What? Then he paused and gestured for Dion to follow.

Together they headed outside. They crossed the car park and walked towards a long, low building. Its front doors were swinging open and shut in the breeze. Dion thought maybe it was some sort of joke, but the manager wasn't laughing as he led the way inside.

The inside was even worse than the outside. There were bottles of cleaning fluid here and there, along with broken furniture and other debris. The floor was covered in rubbish and puddles. There were barely any windows. And the door didn't actually shut. The manager pushed it with his shoulder and it protested as he shoved it into place, but even then there was a large gap at the bottom. A dog Gobi's size would be able to slip right through that space.

"I can't keep her here," Dion argued. "She'd run off."

The manager shrugged. "So?" he said. Then he turned and walked away, back towards the hotel. Dion just watched him go.

"What are we going to do?" Dion wondered aloud.

They were in the car on the way back to Mr Ma's. Lu Xin was driving again, and he and Richard were in the back. "We don't have anywhere else to put her."

He had thought about asking Lu Xin to watch Gobi for him, and he knew that she would if she could. But she lived in a small apartment on the ground floor of a big building. There were too many people coming in and out all the time, and she said it wouldn't be safe. Dion believed her. The last thing he wanted was for Gobi to disappear again.

"I can try to find a place for you to stay with her while you're here," Lu Xin offered from the front and Richard translated. "But it may take a while."

Dion sighed. "It has to be the hotel," he decided. "I need to be able to keep her with me."

"We'll think of something," Richard promised. "We'll make it work."

They drove up to the gate and waited as Mr Ma buzzed them in. A minute later they were pulling up outside the house. Dion had been worried on the way over. What if something had happened to Gobi while he was gone? What if Richard had been right and this was all a scam? What if the Mas hid her again to get more money out of him? But Mr Ma answered the door with a smile, and Dion relaxed.

Then he was inside and headed towards the living room, and there was Gobi. She was okay.

★ ★ ★

When Gobi had woken up that morning, she had been worried. Where was the tall man? But the two men from the night before were here. They seemed nice, and the tall man had been smiling at them, so Gobi figured it was okay. They fed her and gave her water, and she sat and waited. Then she heard a car pull up. There were voices outside. One man went to the front door, and when he came back, the tall man was with him!

★ ★ ★

Gobi yipped and ran straight towards Dion as soon as she saw him. He picked her up and hugged her and she licked his face.

"Yes, I missed you too," he told her. "Don't worry. I'm not leaving again."

He turned back to Mr Ma. "Thank you so much for taking care of her," Dion told Mr Ma and his son. "And for finding her."

"It is our pleasure," Mr Ma replied and Richard translated. Mr Ma's son nodded as well, and he winked at Gobi.

"I'd like to thank you properly," Dion continued. "We are going to have a special dinner tomorrow night for all the people who helped search. I'd like you and your family to come as well. Then I can present you with the reward money."

This time Mr Ma shook his head. "We would be honoured to attend," he replied, bowing. "But I do not need a reward."

It was true that Mr Ma's house was very nice. He and his son looked comfortable and well fed. But Dion was still surprised. "Are you sure?" he asked. "I promised a reward to anyone who found her. And that would be you and your son."

Mr Ma smiled. "You are very kind," he said. "But no thank you."

Dion shrugged. "I can't force you to take the money," he admitted. "But I will bring the cheque anyway, in case you change your mind."

Then Mr Ma's wife came in. She was carrying a tray with tea and pastries. Dion wanted to go back to the hotel with Gobi but knew it would be rude to refuse.

They had already done so much for him. So he sat on the couch again, with Gobi in his lap. Richard sat on one side of him and Lu Xin on the other. The Mas sat across from them, and Mrs Ma poured tea for each of them.

"Thank you," Dion said as he accepted his cup. He took a sip. It was good tea and very strong. "I never asked what you do for a living," he said to Mr Ma.

Their host smiled. "I work in jade," he replied.

"Oh, you're a sculptor?" Dion had seen jade pieces in museums. They were always a beautiful shade of green, and milky rather than clear.

But the Mas laughed. "No," Mr Ma corrected. "I mean I deal in jade. I buy and sell it. For art and other uses."

"Ah. Sorry." Dion smiled. He felt even better about the Mas now. They obviously didn't need the reward money. That meant Richard had been wrong about this being a scam. Or at least the Mas finding Gobi wasn't part of it. He still didn't know about how Gobi had got loose in the first place.

They sat and talked a little longer, then rose to go. But just as they were getting ready to leave, another man entered the house. Dion thought he looked familiar, but couldn't figure out why.

The man marched over to Dion. "Hello," he said, holding out his hand. "I am Nurali's husband."

Dion shook hands with him. "Hi," Dion said back. Nurali's husband laughed, and that was when Dion recognised him. He had been one of the drivers for the race. Not the one whose car Dion had climbed into though.

The man released Dion's hand and turned to study Gobi. He knelt down and picked her up. She didn't growl, but she didn't lick or squeal either.

"Yes," Nurali's husband declared. He turned Gobi around in his hands like he was studying her from every side. "This is Gobi, all right."

Then he handed her to Dion. "We tried our best to keep her safe for you," he said. "But she escaped. She's going to need a good fence when you get her home."

Dion didn't know what to say to that, so he just nodded.

"Let's go," Richard said beside him. Dion nodded. Together they collected Lu Xin, said goodbye to the Mas, and left. Dion glanced back as they walked out to see Mr Ma's son smile back.

Then they were out the door, and Dion breathed a sigh of relief.

Now they just had to figure out how he could get Gobi into the hotel with him.

CHAPTER SEVENTEEN

"This is never going to work," Dion complained as they got out of Lu Xin's car.

Richard grinned. "It will work," he insisted. "Trust me."

Dion shook his head, but finally he sighed. "Okay," he said. "I guess we'll give it a go."

After all, he didn't have any better ideas.

The two of them approached the glass doors of the hotel's front entrance. The armed guards standing there eyed them but made no move to stop them from entering the building. Past those two men stood two more on either side of a metal detector.

Dion hesitated when he saw the guards. He had gone back and forth past them several times – but this would be the first time he was trying to do something criminal.

"Go," Richard hissed behind him, and Dion took a long, lurching step forward. He wobbled on his feet a bit, and the heavy, unzipped duffel bag slung over his shoulder slipped free.

"No!" Dion shouted, lunging for the bag. But there was simply no way he could get to it in time.

The bag hit the ground, falling completely open – and out spilled a huge pile of posters and snacks. Papers, chips, cookies, and nuts went everywhere.

Dion moaned, dropping to his knees and grabbing the bag. "I'm really sorry," he told the guards and the hotel staff who were hurrying over. "Don't worry, I'll pick it all up. I'm really, really sorry." He started scooping up posters and shoving them back into the bag.

Several of the hotel staff started to help him gather everything. The guards didn't bother to help. They were laughing, however. This was probably the funniest thing they had seen in a while. Richard walked right past them and they barely even noticed him.

Finally Dion had everything back in the bag. He rose to his feet, thanked everyone for their help, apologised again, and then stepped through the metal detector. It didn't beep, and with a wave at the guard Dion headed for the elevator.

Richard was already there, and together they waited

for the next elevator. Richard was carrying a bag too, but his was a little smaller. It also matched his coat so well that it was difficult to notice.

They rode up to Dion's room together. Once they were both inside, Dion tossed his bag on the bed and took the smaller bag from Richard. Setting that bag down more gently, he carefully unzipped the side that had been closed. Then Dion reached in and lifted Gobi out.

"So, what did you think?" he asked her. "Your first elevator ride, far as I know. Did you like it?"

Gobi licked his cheek in reply.

Dion laughed. "I'll take that as a yes," he said.

★ ★ ★

Gobi had enjoyed the ride in the funny bag and the strange box that moved up towards the sky. And then when it stopped the doors had opened and they had stepped back out, but everything was different. Before, it had been a big, open space with lots of people standing about. Now it was much narrower and darker and there were doors on both sides. They stopped at one door, and the tall man pulled something out of his pocket. He fitted it into a strange hole in the door, twisted, and suddenly the door swung open. Then they were in a room, the two of them and the other man she remembered and liked from the race. And finally the tall man pulled her out of the bag. Yes!

★ ★ ★

"What now?" Dion wondered as he sank down on to the hotel bed with Gobi in his lap.

Richard shrugged. "Lie low," he suggested. "We've got that dinner tomorrow night, but nothing between now and then. So just relax. Get some sleep. Hang out with Gobi." He ruffled her fur. "Call me if you need anything."

"I will. Thanks." Dion watched his friend go. Then he turned to Gobi. "Looks like it's just you and me," he told her. He reached for the television remote. "Want to watch some TV? I should warn you, though, we only get two channels."

Gobi didn't seem to mind. She curled up beside him on the bed and quickly fell asleep. Dion laughed. He wished he could nap that easily!

Then he switched on the TV and turned the volume down so he wouldn't wake her.

★ ★ ★

The rest of the day was nice and quiet. Dion fell asleep for a while as well. When he and Gobi both woke up, he balled up some of his socks and tossed them so she would have something to chase and wrestle and bite. He set out some water for her, and some food. And whenever she started to look anxious he tucked her back into the bag and took the elevator down to the basement car park to let her relieve herself. He had planned to just take her to a back corner, well away from any cars. But once they were down there he caught sight of the car park exit. Were those bushes by it? He approached carefully, with Gobi at his side. They were! The hotel had planted a small patch of bushes right by the exit, probably to match the plants that lined the walk and the front lawn outside. That was much better than making her relieve herself on bare concrete, or against a wall! Dion gave Gobi a little privacy while she went, but stayed close by. The last thing they needed was someone driving in and spotting her. No one did, and they made it back upstairs without incident.

Gobi seemed perfectly happy with this arrangement. She didn't bark once and seemed fine with riding in the bag. After all the stress of losing her and looking for her, it was nice to have a day of peace and quiet with just the two of them.

* * *

The next morning, though, Dion realised that he had a small problem. He had all the food he'd got for Gobi the other day – but nothing for himself. And he was starving!

She was still asleep on the bed, snoring and twitching like always. Dion hated to wake her up. Surely he could go downstairs, grab some food, and get back before she woke up?

He decided to risk it. Stepping carefully out of the room, he put the Do Not Disturb sign on the handle and then gently closed the door. Whew!

It took him less than fifteen minutes to go downstairs, get some food, and come back up. But when he returned he was surprised to see a housekeeping trolley on his floor.

Then he saw that the door to his room was open.

"Gobi!" he shouted, forgetting all about the need to be quiet. The need to find Gobi was a whole lot stronger.

Charging into the room, Dion checked the bed first. Empty. Then he scanned the rest of the room. Also empty. He was about to run down to the lobby when he noticed that the bathroom door was shut.

Strange. He was sure he had left that open.

Very carefully he opened the door.

There, wiping down the bathroom counter, was one of the hotel maids.

And sitting in the bath tub watching her was Gobi. Who looked very entertained by all this. Her tail was wagging furiously, and she panted at Dion when she spotted him. But she still didn't bark, nor did she get ready to leave her new perch. Instead, after wiggling her eyebrows at Dion, she hunkered down and went back to watching the maid.

Evidently what she was doing was a whole lot more interesting than even chasing after Dion's socks.

Dion tried talking to the maid, but quickly gave up. He had wanted to explain how much trouble he'd be in if anyone found out he had Gobi up here with him. But she didn't speak any English, and he didn't speak Uighur or Chinese.

Finally he pulled out his wallet and handed her a one-hundred-yuan note. That was only fifteen dollars back home. Then he mimed not saying anything about Gobi. The maid nodded. Whether she actually knew what he'd said or not was a whole other story. Right now, she wasn't running downstairs to tell the manager that Dion had smuggled a dog into his room. That would have to be enough.

Privately, Dion suspected that Gobi would get sick of being stuck in this hotel room for days or even weeks on end. But it did give the two of them a chance to recover a little.

He checked out the scar on her head. It looked like it was finally starting to heal. "What – or who – did this to you?" Dion asked her, brushing fur away from the scar a little.

Eventually the maid finished cleaning. "Thank you," Dion said and meant it. He watched as she collected all of her cleaning gear and headed for the door.

It was only after she'd left that Dion wedged some of the couch cushions against the door to the hall. This way they wouldn't rattle every time the ground shook from people walking by or the elevator running and alarm Gobi into barking. As long as no one else tried to get into his room, he and Gobi were all set.

CHAPTER EIGHTEEN

Dion spent the rest of the morning doing interviews by phone whilst Gobi was on the bed sleeping. Newspapers and news sites back in Britain and America had been asking him for updates all along, but Dion had found it difficult to talk to them with Gobi missing. What could he say beyond the note on the crowd-funding site? He didn't know any more about how long she had been missing or how she had got loose or where she was. Having to talk about that over and over again would have been depressing, for him and for all of the people rooting for him and Gobi. Dion hadn't wanted that.

But now things were different. Now he and Gobi were together again. Now he could happily tell the whole story about coming back to China, about searching, and about finding her. He could relax and smile and talk about how they could now move forward with their plan to bring Gobi back to Scotland with him.

Eventually, Gobi woke up. She stretched and yawned, then hopped down out of his lap and padded over to the door. She scratched at it with one paw, not hard, but more to get Dion's attention. Then she whined.

Uh-oh. Dion knew what that meant. She needed to relieve herself. But this wasn't the museum from the storm. There weren't any fake trees right outside the door.

Still, he knew she needed to go. And he couldn't make her go in here. That wasn't fair to Gobi or to the housecleaners.

Which meant he had to take her outside. Outside the room, at least. Dion thought the best bet was to go down to the basement car park again. That was still a little gross, but at least it wasn't in the hall or the room or the lobby! It also meant he didn't have to get past the guards again. But he was still worried. What if the cleaning lady had told someone about Gobi being in his room?

Stepping over to the door, Dion patted Gobi on the head. "I know, girl," he told her. "I know." He took a deep breath, then cracked the door open. Nobody else was out in the hall. "Okay, let's go," he told her, and stepped out. She quickly followed. He had considered hiding her in the bag again, but that had taken a lot of effort the first time. He didn't think it would be worth it for such a quick trip.

They trotted over to the elevator, and Dion pushed the Down button. The whole time they were waiting, he kept glancing around. What would he do if someone else came out into the hall? It wasn't like he could hide Gobi then! If the guest was a foreigner like him, they might not mind. In fact, they might even know who he was and who Gobi was. But if they were Chinese he would be in trouble. There was no way they would be happy about discovering that a dog was sharing their floor!

Fortunately, no one else emerged. The elevator dinged, and when it finally opened, it was empty. Dion hurried in, with Gobi beside him. He pressed the button for the car park, and the doors slid shut.

No one else got on, and they reached the car park without any problem. "Not ideal, I know," Dion told Gobi as they walked across it. "But I hope it's okay for now." She didn't complain, at least.

They headed for the exit and the same patch of bushes as before. Again Dion turned his back to give

Gobi some privacy. He heard the elevator ding and glanced that way. It opened and two men in dark suits came out. Dion worried that they might be headed his way, but instead they turned and got into a grey saloon. "Time to go, Gobi," he urged. If the car came this way, the men would see her for sure.

Fortunately, when he glanced over his shoulder Gobi had finished. She kicked some dirt back over what she'd left, and then trotted to his side, her tail wagging.

Dion led her away from the exit but not straight back towards the elevator. Instead he circled around so that the grey saloon wouldn't see them as it passed.

But as they were walking, he heard the elevator again. This time only one man exited, but Dion's heart sank. It was a security guard. And the man stationed himself in front of the elevator, arms crossed.

Now what were they going to do? Dion had no idea how long the security guard planned to stand there. It could be all day! Or he might start walking around the car park to make sure the cars were safe and no one had snuck in from outside. Either way, they would get caught.

Dion thought about calling Richard for help. Maybe he could come down here and distract the security guard so Dion could sneak Gobi back on to the elevator? But there weren't any places to hide here, really. The guard would probably see them, and then there would be trouble.

Finally Dion decided that the best option was the direct one. "Come on, Gobi," he said, and headed straight for the elevator.

The security guard watched him approach. The man straightened and nodded at Dion. But then he spotted Gobi and held up his hand for them to stop.

Dion did stop, just a few feet from the man, and Gobi stopped at his side, as always. "We're just heading back up to our room," he explained. Dion had no idea if the guard understood him, so he pulled out his room key and held that up. Then he pointed at the elevator.

The guard pointed at Gobi and shook his head. That was exactly what Dion had been afraid of. He frowned. What could he do now? Beside him, Gobi cocked her head to one side. It didn't look like she had any answers either.

Then Dion remembered the maid. Reaching into his pocket, he pulled out another one-hundred-yuan note and held it up. Then he waved it towards the elevator.

The guard considered that for a moment. Finally he

nodded. Dion handed him the money, and the guard stepped aside to let them pass. Both of them.

"Well, that was lucky," Dion said after the elevator door had closed behind them, and he and Gobi were alone.

He was still worried, though. What if the guard told the hotel manager about Gobi? What if he told someone else? What if the maid told someone? The more people who knew he had Gobi here, the more likely it was that someone would come to disturb them.

Dion hoped that Lu Xin found a place for them soon.

★ ★ ★

Gobi didn't know exactly what was going on. But she wasn't worried. The tall man had taken her to this funny house with all the floors and the moving box and the basement filled with cars. It was a strange place, but nice. They had a room that was bigger than the tent they had shared with the other runners. They had a bathroom. They had food and water and a comfy couch and a comfy bed. And they were together. So Gobi was happy.

Then she heard someone outside. There were footsteps, followed by a knock on the door. Gobi sniffed. She knew that scent! She started barking. *Go away!* she said.

★ ★ ★

The knock on the door surprised Dion, but he was more startled when Gobi started barking. He'd never heard her do that before.

"Shhh," he warned her, and she stopped at once. But if anyone else had heard her, it was already too late.

Dion crossed to the door and looked through the peephole. Two men stood outside. One of them was Nurali's husband.

What do they want? Dion thought.

And how had they even found him?

There was only one way out of the room, and that was the door between Dion and the men. And the men had heard her barking, so Dion couldn't pretend they weren't here.

He took out his phone, pulled up Richard's number and texted: "Come to my room immediately."

The other man outside the door was raising his hand to knock again. Dion didn't want to risk any other guests wondering what all the noise was about and hearing Gobi as well, so he opened the door just enough to peer out.

"Hello?" he said. He tried to smile and look relaxed but wasn't sure he was very convincing.

Nurali's husband just stared at him. "Can we come in?" he asked.

For a second, Dion considered saying no and slamming the door. But he knew he couldn't do that – anyway he was curious to know what they wanted.

"Okay," Dion said finally, and stepped back to let them enter.

Dion shut the door once the men were inside. He turned to find them standing over Gobi, staring down at her. She didn't seem frightened, and she wasn't barking any more.

Someone knocked on his door, and Dion jumped. But when he checked, he felt better. It was Richard.

"Hey, man, what do you need?" Richard asked as Dion opened the door again.

"Um, yes, mate," Dion mumbled. He swung the door all the way open, so Richard could see into the room. "Didn't you want to come and get some of those posters to take home as souvenirs?" he asked. It was a weak excuse and he knew it. He was sure Nurali's husband thought it odd that Richard had just turned up.

Fortunately, Richard saw what was happening and played along. "Oh, yeah, right," he agreed. He nodded to Nurali's husband and his silent friend. "What's up?" He didn't enter the room though. There wasn't enough space for all of them.

Dion felt a lot better now that Richard was here. His friend was an ex-Marine, after all. More importantly, he could speak Chinese so he could help get to the bottom of this. Now he did step between the two men and pick up Gobi. She licked his face as he held her and turned to face them.

Nurali's husband finally fired off a long sentence in rapid Chinese. Dion didn't understand him, of course. But then the other man spoke and waited for the translation.

Nurali and her husband had seen all the press coverage Gobi had been getting and were worried Dion would blame them for her escape.

That part Dion certainly understood. He nodded. "All I want to do is get Gobi out of here and get back home," he promised them. "I'm not interested in trying to find out how she escaped and I'm not interested in finding someone to blame." He continued, "As far as I'm concerned it was just an accident and it's all fine now."

He stared back at the men. "It's in all our interests to keep it that way too, isn't it?"

Finally Nurali's husband nodded. He shouldered past Dion and Gobi, and his friend followed. Richard shifted from the doorway to let them pass. Dion watched them head to the elevator. He didn't relax until it had arrived and taken them away. Then he finally slumped against the wall.

Richard shook his head. "That was fun," he said.

Dion knew his friend meant the exact opposite, and he agreed. No, it had not been fun at all. But hopefully that was the last they would see of those two.

CHAPTER NINETEEN

That night, Dion left Gobi in their hotel room and went down to the hotel's restaurant. He was treating the entire search team to dinner as a thank-you for all their help.

It felt strange that he had to leave Gobi behind for this event. After all, she was the one he was thanking everyone for! But of course there was no way they could bring her to the restaurant. The hotel still didn't know she was a guest here – or if they did know, they were pretending they didn't. Dion was fine with that. They could say they didn't have a dog in the hotel all they wanted, as long as Gobi could stay with him.

Dinner was very nice, and everyone was in a really good mood. The Mas were there too, and Dion thanked everyone for all their hard work. The volunteers had been amazing, and in the end it had all paid off. That was the best part, that they could celebrate the fact that they had found Gobi.

Dion insisted that the Mas accept the reward money. At first Mr Ma refused. But finally he accepted the cheque. Dion was glad. He had promised to reward whoever found Gobi, and he didn't want to go back on his word.

"I remember when I first heard about Gobi," Lu Xin told him at one point.

"When you were racing," she said. "There aren't many stories on the news about dogs, so whenever there's a story I always follow it." She smiled. "I knew Gobi was special even then, but I never thought I'd get to meet her."

Dion hugged her, this sweet Chinese lady who had helped him so much. "You did more than just get to meet her, Lu Xin," he pointed out. "Without you we wouldn't have found her. You're the reason we're all celebrating tonight."

She blushed but looked pleased. Dion was glad. He had meant what he said. It was amazing to look at all these people and think just how much they had given to help him and Gobi find each other again.

After dinner, Dion went back to his room. He checked on Gobi, who was fine. Then he did a short phone interview with *The Times*. After that he headed back out. Richard was leaving early the next morning, and Dion wanted to see his friend one last time before he left.

Richard had said before that a lot of the story of Gobi's disappearance didn't make sense. That night, he said it again.

"I don't think Gobi ever really escaped," he insisted. "At least, not the way Nurali thought."

Dion frowned. "So what do you think happened?" he asked.

His friend shook his head. "I think when the story started to spread, and the crowd-funding got so big, somebody figured out they could make some money off all this and took her when the opportunity arose. They then hid her and said she'd escaped so that you'd put up a reward for her return. Then they held on to her because the story kept growing, and they figured the reward might increase too."

"Why didn't they ever demand more money, then?" Dion asked.

He was surprised when his friend looked away. Richard seemed embarrassed.

"What?" Dion demanded. "What's going on?"

"That's why Lu Xin got so many calls saying that Gobi was dead already," Richard finally answered. "Or that she was going to be killed unless the reward money increased."

Dion was horrified. Then he stopped. "Wait, what do you mean so many calls?" he asked. "I thought there was just the one phone call? And nobody told me they were asking for more money." He remembered when Lu Xin had got the call. She'd said it was someone saying that Gobi would be killed. Dion had just thought it was some sick joke or something. But it had really been someone saying she would be killed unless they increased the reward.

Richard was shaking his head. "They did ask for more money," he admitted. "And there were hundreds of calls like that. They just didn't want to worry you."

And Richard had apparently known about it all along. Dion was grateful that his friends had kept the truth from him – he wasn't sure he could have handled it. At the same time, he was angry that they had hidden anything from him. Gobi was his dog – he had a right to know!

"So why didn't they keep up with those demands?" he asked now.

His friend smiled. "You came back," Richard answered. "And you got the local press involved. Then the government started getting interested. Local officials even joined the WeChat group you set up. They knew that they couldn't keep Gobi any longer. If they had, and someone had found out, they'd have got in huge trouble. It wasn't worth the risk."

That made sense, Dion thought. He remembered how people would stop him on the street, just to take a picture with him. He had become a local celebrity. If you were the person who stole that celebrity's dog, it wouldn't look good for you. And the government could get angry at someone for making all of them look bad.

Richard hadn't finished. "Don't you think it's weird that Gobi ended up with someone who knew Nurali?" That was true, Dion realised.

"So you think that the Ma family took her?" he asked. They had seemed so nice! But he remembered how Nurali's husband had turned up at the Mas' house, and how he'd been talking to Mr Ma's son when they left.

"No," Richard corrected. "They are rich and do not need the money. Why would they take a dog? But it is a big coincidence that Gobi was left somewhere where people who knew her story could find her." He laughed. "And how, in a city this crowded and this close to mountains and open space, does Gobi wind up in the most expensive gated community for miles around? Did she get spoiled in the time you were gone? It's more likely the kidnappers planted her there."

Dion thought back to the race. Gobi had been perfectly happy sharing an inflatable mattress in a tent with him. She had lived on scraps of food, and water from streams. Richard was right, it didn't make sense for her to have been in that community. Not unless she had been brought there deliberately.

There was nothing he could do about any of it now, of course. Even if it had been a scam, he had promised a reward for Gobi's safe return. She was back, and safe, and he was happy to pay that amount in exchange.

But after talking to Richard, Dion couldn't help wondering if someone else might come and try taking Gobi away from him. Maybe someone would think they could get even more money if she disappeared again.

Well, he wasn't going to let that happen.

Over the next few days, Dion did fifty interviews in person, by phone, or by Skype. Everyone he'd spoken to when Gobi was missing wanted to talk to him now that she was found, and he was happy to share the good news.

Dion did text Lu Xin though. He reminded her about finding them an apartment. The hotel had been very nice, but he couldn't take Gobi in and out easily. He also hadn't brought her to a vet yet, in part because sneaking her in and out was so difficult. It would just be much easier if they were staying somewhere else. And he would feel a lot safer too.

He had just finished texting Lu Xin when someone knocked on the door. Gobi was sound asleep, so Dion got up carefully in order to keep from waking her. He worried that it might be Nurali's husband again. And Richard was no longer here to help.

But it wasn't Nurali's husband.

Instead it was two men in dark suits. Dion recognised them right away. They were the same men he had seen in the car park the other day. The ones with the grey saloon.

What should he do? Gobi hadn't barked, and he

hadn't said anything, so they might not know he was there. If he waited, maybe they would just go away. Dion decided to try that. He stepped away from the door as quietly as he could.

They knocked again.

It wasn't a loud knock, or an angry one. But it was solid. If he'd been asleep, that knock would have woken him up. He was just glad that it hadn't woken Gobi.

Maybe the men weren't here to hurt him or Gobi, Dion thought. Maybe the government had sent them to make sure he was okay. Or maybe they were here for some other reason. But what?

On the other hand, they might be here to demand money. Or to kidnap Gobi. Or just to kick him out of the hotel, though he thought the manager would have done that himself.

Whatever their purpose. Dion didn't want to find out.

So he stood there, not moving, not daring to make a sound.

A minute went by. Nothing. No more knocks. Then another minute. Then another.

After five minutes Dion tiptoed back over to the door and looked through the peephole.

The hall was empty. The men had gone.

Dion could barely breathe. He texted Lu Xin again immediately. "Please get us out of here!" he pleaded. It was definitely time to go.

CHAPTER TWENTY

Dion wanted to just take Gobi straight to Beijing and get out of Urumqi completely. But they still needed to see the vet and get medical approval. Once they had that, Kiki could get Gobi permission to fly. With any luck, they would only be here a few more days.

Fortunately, Lu Xin was able to find Dion and Gobi an apartment that same day.

Dion managed to get Gobi out of the hotel without a problem. He simply took her down to the car park one last time, and handed her over to Lu Xin. Then he went back upstairs, checked out, and left through the front. Lu Xin and Gobi were waiting in Lu Xin's car outside.

They drove to the new apartment. It wasn't fancy at all, but it was clean. There were plenty of shops and restaurants nearby, and the streets were busy but not too crowded. It was perfect.

After Lu Xin left, Dion locked the door. Then he glanced down at Gobi.

"It's quite the adventure we've got ourselves into, isn't it, Gobi?" he said as he ruffled her fur.

★ ★ ★

Gobi looked up at the tall man. This new place smelled a little like cleaning fluid. It was okay though. She had liked the room they had just left, but she hadn't liked being cooped up all the time. This place had more windows and more air. It had a couch and a bed and a table. But more importantly, it had her person. As long as he was with her, she was fine.

She stared up at him for a second. Then she sniffed his feet. Next she trotted over to the couch. Jumping up on it, she turned around a few times to make it more comfortable. Satisfied, she flopped down and curled up to take a nap.

As far as she was concerned, this place was fine.

★ ★ ★

The next day didn't go as smoothly though. Dion had finally got an appointment to take Gobi to the vet. The man was supposed to be one of the top guys in the city, but he was very rough with Gobi. She squealed with pain when he pulled on her injured leg. Afterwards, the vet told Dion that her hip was displaced and her femur had been bent away from the socket. She would need surgery to correct that, he said. But Dion wasn't about to let that man touch her again.

After a short nap back in the apartment, Gobi seemed recovered from the trauma of the vet. Dion took her outside for a walk. They could both use some fresh air, he thought. It was a beautiful day. Several people stopped them for pictures – thanks to all the interviews, everyone seemed to know who Dion and Gobi were. Gobi was happy to meet new people and sat patiently for each picture. Dion didn't mind either. It was nice to make people smile.

But at one point Dion looked around – and saw a familiar car parked nearby. It was the grey saloon from the hotel car park. He could make out the two men in dark suits sitting inside.

He knew that couldn't be a coincidence. They must

have followed him here from the hotel. How long had they been watching him and Gobi? Who were they, exactly? And what did they want?

Part of him wanted to march right over and demand answers. But what if they were here to hurt him or Gobi? There were two of them. And Dion wasn't a fighter.

Instead, he turned and headed back towards the apartment. There wasn't any point in running or in pretending he was going somewhere else. It was clear the men knew exactly where he lived.

Gobi didn't complain that their walk had been cut short. She just trotted along beside Dion, the same as always. If she picked up on his fear, she didn't show it.

As Dion was closing the apartment door behind him, the phone rang. He jumped. Was it the men from the grey saloon? He considered letting it ring, but decided to take a chance and answer it.

"Hello?" he said.

"Dion?" a man said on the other end. "It's Wendy."

It took Dion a second to realise who she was. Then he remembered. Wendy was an international Freelance journalist living in Hong Kong and knew Lu Xin. They had spoken once or twice. Wendy had been helping Kiki make arrangements for when Dion brought Gobi to Beijing.

"Hey," Dion said finally. "Hi."

"Are you okay?" she asked. "You sound odd."

"Yeah. No. Maybe," Dion replied. "There are these guys following me." He told Wendy about the men in the dark suits.

"That's actually why I'm calling," Wendy said. "It's not just the guys in the car." She didn't sound surprised at all. "You've got some pretty big people watching this, Dion."

Dion frowned. "What do you mean?" he asked. He was still trying to figure out why Wendy didn't sound more concerned.

"Just that," she answered. "You've got to be careful what you say." She lowered her voice like she didn't want anyone to overhear. "I've spoken to some colleagues, as they've heard that there are some local government advisors who are watching the story and listening to everything you say."

"You've got to make sure that anything you say about China is said in a positive way," Wendy warned.

Dion sat down on the couch. He closed his eyes

and tried to wrap his head around what Wendy had said. "You've talked to people about this?" he asked after a second. "You mean that someone's told you this?"

"Don't worry about how, Dion. I just wanted to make sure you got the message." Dion understood.

Dion's thoughts went back to the men in the dark suits. "So you think these guys in the suits are from the state?" he asked.

"Well, they're not there to steal Gobi, are they?" Wendy pointed out.

No, Dion realised. They weren't. If they had been after Gobi, they could have done it any time.

They also could have done a better job hiding, he thought.

"They're here for my protection?" he wondered aloud.

"Kind of," Wendy agreed. "As long as you do the right thing you'll be fine. Just don't talk to CNN again."

"CNN?" Dion glanced up. "How do you know about CNN?" He had actually had one interview with them already. They had asked him to do a second one, and he had been trying to arrange a time for that.

Wendy didn't explain. She only said, "There's bad blood between CNN and the Chinese state. Just steer clear, okay?"

Dion promised he'd be careful. He even remembered to thank Wendy for the warning. Then he hung up and sat there, stunned.

Is this my life now? he thought. It was more like a bad spy movie! Men following him, other men threatening him, plots to scam money from him – how had all of this happened?

But she hadn't sounded panicked. She had told Dion everything would be all right. She had also said that Dion was doing fine so far. That was a good thing.

Dion did cancel his plans for a second CNN interview. And, just to be sure, he turned down several other requests for overseas interviews. He even told Lu Xin that he didn't want to talk to any Chinese media either. It was better to play it safe, he decided. He didn't want to risk saying the wrong thing to the wrong person and losing Gobi forever.

She had been sitting beside him throughout the phone calls. Now she whined and licked his face. Then she hopped into his lap and curled up there.

"Don't worry," Dion assured the little dog softly as he petted her. "Yes, it's all a bit nuts. But you're worth it."

CHAPTER TWENTY-ONE

Dion and Gobi spent several more days in the apartment. They didn't see the men in the dark suits again, though Dion guessed that they were probably still watching from somewhere nearby. But Dion had decided not to let fear stop him and Gobi from enjoying themselves as much as they could. They took long walks, they played and napped, and Dion even made friends with some of the locals when he stepped out one night to get some food.

But finally they were ready to go. Kiki had worked her magic and we were flying to Beijing tomorrow. Kiki had come out to Urumqi to make sure everything went smoothly. Dion was glad she was there, especially when they headed to the airport. Gobi already looked unhappy about being stuck inside a crate. Dion hated to think how she'd look after a three-hour flight spent in the cargo hold.

"We don't have a choice," Kiki had explained to Dion. "There's simply no way Gobi can fly in the cabin with you." Dion knew that was true. Here in China they were oddly suspicious of dogs. Some people had even crossed the street when they'd seen him out walking Gobi. Kiki was right, they would never let Gobi fly with him.

"Take care down there," Dion told Gobi as he settled her into the crate. He'd added an old T-shirt so she would have something that smelled like him, and she had food and water and a cushion to lie on. All in all, it was a nice, cosy little space. The question was, how would Gobi cope with altitudes, especially when they were mixed with speed and cold. There was nothing else Dion could do though. In order to get back home they would have to fly from either Shanghai or Beijing, and that meant flying to one of those two cities first. Besides, he decided that it was better to know beforehand how Gobi would handle being on a plane. This way, if there were any problems he and Kiki could figure out ways to help Gobi handle travelling better when it was time to finally leave China.

★ ★ ★

Gobi whined and whimpered. She did not like this at all! The crate itself was not so bad – she was used to being able to roam at will, but at least there was enough room to turn around in here. And it had a comfy bed, and food and water, and the tall man – her person – had put one of his shirts in here so it even smelled like him.

But she did not like being in this busy, noisy, smelly, crowded place! There were just too many people, and she couldn't run and hide. True, she had the crate to protect her, but what if they got in somehow? She would have nowhere to go!

Then some men put her crate on a strange shelf that moved, and it carried her away! The tall man and the nice lady disappeared, and everything was dark! That passed eventually, and Gobi found herself in a large, noisy room that smelled of metal. All the people here were rushing around, and some of them grabbed her crate and moved it on to a covered trolley. That drove out on to a big, open space, and Gobi barked when she saw the sky again. Maybe the journey was over? If so, it had not been nearly as bad as she thought!

But no. Instead of taking her back to her person, or even releasing her, the men drove the trolley over to a big metal box sitting out in the open. Then they loaded her crate and a bunch of other boxes and bags into the bottom of the box! It was dark in here, and chilly, and

Gobi barked and barked. All the men did was secure her crate with some straps and then leave her there. She was all alone!

And it got worse. After a little while, the box shook and made loud clanking noises. Then there was a steady, almost deafening roar. And then the whole box started moving! Gobi could tell it was moving fast too, faster than she could run, maybe faster than a car. Then there was a strange floating sensation, and the world tilted. She fell down but fortunately landed on her bed. Some of her water spilled, though, and her food.

When they finally righted again, it was so cold! Gobi could see her breath every time she gasped. She barked but nobody came, and finally she gave up and hunkered down on her bed with a whimper. This was horrible! She finally fell asleep, but it wasn't restful. She kept tossing and turning.

When would this nightmare be over?

★ ★ ★

Sadly, Gobi turned out not to like flying – at least, not in the cargo hold. By the time Dion was able to retrieve her crate after the flight, the inside looked like it had been put through a blender. The water bottle had been smashed, the leash had been chewed through, the food was scattered everywhere, and Gobi was snapping and shivering and staring, wide-eyed, all around her. *That was probably her first flight ever*, Dion realised as he spotted Kiki by the door and waved. She returned the gesture, and motioned for them join her.

"Good flight?" Kiki asked as soon as they were all together. She glanced into Gobi's pen and sighed. "No, I can see that at least one of you didn't enjoy the flight at all." She led the way towards the car park, where she had left her truck. "Well, you're here now. You made it!"

As soon as they were in the truck Dion released the catches on the crate door. Gobi leaped into his arms, and he held her and petted her until her shivering stopped. "You're okay," he promised her over and over again. "You made it. It's all right."

But of course he knew that this was really just the beginning of their journey.

"I've got a space all set up for her," Kiki promised as she drove out of the airport car park and on to the streets of Beijing. "She'll be comfy, I promise. And I'll be here in Beijing the whole time – I'll stop by to see her every day, even if I'm not in the office that day."

Gobi had to spend the next month here in Beijing while they got her another round of medical approvals and waited for permission to take her out of the country completely. She would be staying at Kiki's boarding kennels, and Dion knew she would take good care of Gobi. He smiled as Kiki reached over and ruffled the little dog's fur. It was obvious that Kiki loved animals, and clear that she already liked Gobi in particular. And Gobi liked her too – the little dog licked her hand, which made Kiki laugh. They would be fine together, he was sure.

That didn't make leaving the next day any easier, though. It broke Dion's heart when he said goodbye to Gobi. She obviously knew something was up, because she whimpered and whined and pressed against his leg like she was urging him not to go. "I'll be back, I promise," he told her, scooping her up into a final hug. "You'll stay with Kiki for a month, then I'll come to get you again and we'll head home." Except that they wouldn't be able to go straight home, he knew. He would come back so that he could fly Gobi to London, but then she would have to spend the next four months in quarantine in Heathrow. He didn't want to think about that right now though. They had made it to Beijing, which was the first step. He just had to focus on that.

Dion tried not to look back as he headed for the door. And he tried not to hear Gobi whimpering behind him. It was the same noise she had made that day of the race, when they had reached the river and he had started across without her.

But this time he knew he couldn't turn around and go to get her. It just didn't work that way. "I'll see you in a month," he told her instead.

Then he hurried out the door, trying not to cry.

CHAPTER TWENTY-TWO

Dion's flight home was rough. Not because there were any problems on the flight itself, but because he was busy thinking.

He was excited to see Lucja again, of course. It had been two weeks, and even though they had talked on the phone many times, it wasn't the same.

He was also pleased to be going back to work. His boss had been great about letting him take extra time to go back to look for Gobi. His co-workers had been supportive as well. But his being gone meant they had been forced to do extra work. Not one of them had complained about it, but Dion didn't want to push that. He needed to prove to them and his boss that they could still rely on him.

But he was sad about leaving Gobi behind. It was more than that though. He was also worried.

Not about how she would do with Kiki. Dion knew

Gobi would miss him, but that Kiki would take good care of her. He had complete trust in that.

No, he was worried about what would happen after the thirty days were up. He would have to go back to get Gobi, of course – the rules required that he be the one to bring her home. But it was a really long flight from Beijing to London. And Britain did not allow dogs to fly into the country in the passenger cabin, which meant Gobi would be stuck in the hold again.

Then there was the quarantine. Leaving her at Heathrow was their only option – there was no other place in Britain that would hold pets during that process. Gobi would hate being stuck there. And it would be hard for Dion and Lucja to visit her. They could probably only manage to get down there on weekends, and even then only for a few hours. But it was actually recommended that the pet owners not visit their pets in quarantine. It apparently made it harder for the pets to see them leave each time, which meant Dion was supposed to just leave Gobi alone in a strange place for four months. He wasn't sure he could handle that – or that she could.

But there was another option Kiki had brought up

after they had reached her boarding kennels. She'd seen how upset Gobi had been after the flight from Urumqi.

"She can stay here with me for a month, and then fly to London and spend another four months there," Kiki had explained. "Or she can just stay here in Beijing. She'd have to be cleared of rabies – we do a blood test for one month first and then we wait another three months before another final blood test before you leave. But after that, as long she has all of her paperwork in order, you could take her home and actually fly her directly to Edinburgh. She would never have to go into quarantine at all."

That was an amazing possibility. But Dion knew that there was no way he could ask Kiki to hold Gobi for four months. That wasn't fair to her, especially after she had already been so helpful. Besides, what if someone tried to take Gobi away again? People were still asking for constant updates on the site. If someone decided to steal her and hold her for another reward, Dion wouldn't even be here to help. And although he trusted Kiki, he didn't know everyone who would be in and out of her kennel.

That left one other option. Dion liked it, but he

knew he would have to convince Lucja and his boss. If either of them said no, he was stuck.

"I want to stay with her," Dion told Lucja the night after he got home. It was amazing to see his wife again, and to tell her in person everything that had happened. But now he had told her about the quarantine, and the other option, and his plan. "If I go back there now, Kiki said she can help me find an apartment. I'll stay with Gobi and then the two of us can come back home together."

He waited and watched his wife as she considered this. She hadn't said no right away, he thought. That was a good sign.

Finally, she sighed. "I'll miss you, of course," she told him. She smiled. "But I'll manage. And I know a certain little dog who will be very, very happy."

Dion stared at her. "You mean it?" he asked after a second. "You're okay with this?"

Lucja laughed and hugged him. "We've been married for years," she pointed out. "I think I'll survive without you for a few more months. But for Gobi, that's practically a lifetime. She needs you more than I do. And then you'll bring her home, and we'll all be together for good." She kissed him. "So yes, I'm okay with it."

Dion felt like cheering. Instead he laughed, and cried a little, and kissed her back. "I don't know what I'd do without you," he told her. Then he sighed. "Now I just need to see about work."

Dion had called his boss as soon as he arrived home. He told them he was back, and that he would be coming in tomorrow. But he also admitted that he was worried about leaving Gobi back in China. He mentioned all the strange things that had happened in Urumqi, and Richard's theories about Gobi's disappearance being a scam for the reward money. Then he explained the situation with the quarantine, and his plan to go back to spend those four months with Gobi instead.

"I know I've put you through a lot with all this," he said, "and I know it's not fair for me to just disappear again. So if you want me to resign, I will. That way you can find someone else and have a full staff again."

"No," his boss said. "I appreciate the offer, but you're not going to resign. Come and see me tomorrow." Then he hung up.

So the next day, after Lucja had given her approval, Dion went in to work. It was great to see all his co-workers again. Everyone asked about Gobi, and about the trip. Dion had taken plenty of pictures and was happy to show them off – not just photos of Gobi, but of the area, of their apartment, and of the friends he had made there. Then he went in to see his boss.

"You're going on sabbatical," his boss informed him once they were both seated. "For six months."

"What?" Dion couldn't believe his ears. A sabbatical was basically an extended holiday. You didn't get paid for that time, but it also meant you returned to work after it was over. But he hadn't applied for a sabbatical – usually those were reserved for real emergencies!

His boss smiled. "It's okay," he said. "I rushed it through. This way you can focus on Gobi. Go back there, be with her, make sure she's okay, and bring her home safe. Your job will be here for you when you get back."

Dion didn't know what to say, except, "Thank you so much. This means the world to me." And it did. He had always liked his job, and his co-workers, and his boss. He had been here for eleven years, after all! But this was absolutely amazing, and he had never expected such generosity. And to know that he could go back to China without having to worry about work was just incredible.

Dion left work that day full of hope and happiness. So many people had helped him and Lucja along the way. He knew he was incredibly lucky to have such support. And that Gobi was lucky too.

Now he just had a return trip to plan.

Dion flew back to China a few days later. He had only been home for a week. But this time it would be a lot longer before he came back. And when he did, he wouldn't be alone.

Kiki met him at the airport. She had a big grin on her face as she led him back to her truck. Dion found out why the second he got in and a small brown shape launched herself at him. "Somebody sure missed you," Kiki said with a laugh as Gobi covered Dion in kisses.

"Well, I missed her too," Dion replied, hugging his dog. She looked great. It was clear that Kiki had taken good care of her. "I guess this is where you and I start our new life together," he told Gobi.

She stared back at him, her eyes locked on his. And Dion was absolutely sure that she understood what he meant.

Kiki had found them a small apartment on the eleventh floor of a building. Dion was fine with that.

He and Gobi didn't need much, and being so high up made him feel safer. They spent the next four months together, exploring the area. A lot of places wouldn't let him in if he had Gobi with him, but others were much nicer about it. Kiki helped Dion register ownership of Gobi and get an official licence. That was good too. He felt much safer knowing he could now prove that she was his. They spent a lot of time walking outside, at least until the weather changed. On 15th November, the government turned on the heating nationwide, but that caused a huge jump in pollution. The air quality got so bad it was dangerous to go outside, which left Dion and Gobi cooped up in their small apartment. Gobi was cleared of rabies but then got kennel cough from being stuck inside so much. She recovered quickly, though. Dion also took her to a new vet to get an operation for her damaged hip. That hurt her a great deal, and Dion found that he couldn't bear to watch. But within a day Gobi was feeling better, and soon she was able to walk and run without any pain, just like when he had first met her.

Right after Gobi's operation, Dion got a call from a journalist he'd met in Urumqi. "There's a race," he explained. "It's only a single-stage, but it's here in the

Gobi Desert again. The organisers are gathering fifty of the world's best sixty-mile runners. Are you interested?"

Dion didn't have think about that for long. He had wanted to get back to racing again, but hadn't been able to because of everything with Gobi. He had actually backed out of one race he had signed up for because he had been busy searching for her. But this race was only one day, and it was here in China. Plus, the organisers offered to pay for his trip and his hotel if he took part and also met with journalists. His story with Gobi meant that his being in the race would bring them some extra publicity.

Dion checked with Kiki. "Of course I'll take care of her while you're gone," she promised. "I'll totally pamper her here. It'll be like a vacation for her too."

Dion agreed to the race. And then it got even better. "We still have a few spaces available," the organisers told him a few days before the event. "We're willing to fly out any other elite runners who want to compete. Do you know anybody?"

"Absolutely," Dion replied. And then he called Lucja.

Only six weeks earlier, she had run three hundred miles, over five days, across Holland. And she didn't have much time to prepare for this event, but she said yes anyway.

A sandstorm struck when they were more than halfway through the race. A lot of people gave up, but not Dion and Lucja. They kept running. When they crossed the finish line together, hand in hand, Dion told her, "Happy anniversary." They had been married eleven years ago that day. It was a great way for them to celebrate.

Lucja stayed one night in Beijing before heading back. And when Kiki picked them up at the airport, Dion wasn't the only one Gobi licked. She took to Lucja immediately, and Dion was happy to see that the feeling was mutual. By the time Lucja left the next morning, he knew that Gobi had won her heart as well.

CHAPTER TWENTY-THREE

It was more than a month before Dion and Gobi saw Lucja again. But she returned a few days before Christmas to help them prepare. It was almost time for them to go.

Lucja didn't stay long this time either. She still had a lot to check and prepare on the other end of the trip. But this time when they said goodbye Dion knew he would see her again very soon. And so would Gobi.

Dion and Gobi's flight out was on New Year's Eve. But it wasn't to London, or even to Edinburgh. Because after the flight to Beijing had upset her so much, Dion had decided he wouldn't ever let them put Gobi in the cargo hold again.

That was a problem, though. Because that meant he couldn't fly into Britain with her. They had to find a different route home.

Dion, Lucja, and Kiki came up with a plan. Dion

and Gobi would fly from Beijing to Paris instead. That was still a ten-hour flight, but France didn't have the same restrictions for dogs on planes. Gobi would be able to travel with Dion instead of with the luggage. Lucja would be waiting for them in Paris, and then the three of them would drive to Amsterdam. That was another five hours. From there they would take an overnight ferry to Newcastle, which would take almost twelve hours. After that they just had the two-and-a-half hour drive back home to Edinburgh. All in all, the trip would take forty-one hours. But if it kept Gobi from panicking, it was worth every second.

Kiki picked Dion and Gobi up and drove them to the airport. They ran into some trouble checking in, though.

"Did you book Gobi on the flight?" Kiki asked Dion after arguing with the check-in lady in Chinese.

Dion shook his head. "I didn't do it," he said. "I thought you were doing it."

But Kiki shook her head as well. "Lucja supposed to do it."

Dion called Lucja, but she said, "No, Kiki was supposed to do it."

Obviously there had been a mix-up. According to

the check-in lady, it was now too late to get Gobi into the system. She couldn't go on the plane.

Dion had to force himself to stay calm. Gobi's paperwork was only good for travel through to 2nd January. If they missed this flight, they would have to get permission all over again. Who knew how long that would take?

Fortunately, a second check-in clerk arrived. And then a third. The third one was clearly in charge. He listened to Kiki, then said something in reply. "Go to that counter there," Kiki translated for Dion. She pointed to a nearby Air France check-in counter. "Pay two hundred dollars and he says they will get her on board."

Dion was stunned. Hadn't they said it was impossible?

But Kiki smiled. "I told them Gobi is a famous dog," she explained. "They know story and wanted to make it happen for you."

Dion was grateful. The check-in staff wanted to take selfies with him and Gobi, and Dion was happy to agree. It was a small price to pay for their fixing the problem.

It took some time to clear customs as well. They inspected Dion's things and then said they had to check

Gobi as well. But finally the phone in the customs office rang. The guard answered it, listened, then nodded. "Okay," he told Dion. "Dog cleared to fly. You go."

And Dion went.

They boarded the plane without any more trouble, and Dion was even able to sit Gobi on the seat next to him. She had to stay in the carry bag Dion had bought for her, but since she was next to him she didn't seem to mind too much.

★ ★ ★

Gobi had been nervous. This was like that loud place they had been in once before! But instead of a crate she was in a soft bag, and nobody tried taking her away from her person. Instead they were shown to a pair of seats in a strange, shiny room. Gobi heard noises like she had last time, the clanks and the roars and everything else. But it was a lot less scary when you could see and when there were other people around. None of them seemed worried, including the tall man. So Gobi decided that she shouldn't worry either. Especially once he picked up her bag and set it on his lap. A little while later, they turned down the lights. People all around them were asleep. Then her person unzipped the bag and quietly lifted Gobi out. He cradled her in his arms, and she fell asleep, warm and safe.

★ ★ ★

Lucja was waiting for them at Charles de Gaulle Airport in Paris. Both Dion and Gobi were happy to see her, and together they drove to Amsterdam. Lucja's aunt, uncle, and cousins lived there, so they stopped off for a brief visit.

Next they headed to the ferry, but there was a problem there as well.

"We can't read this," the woman at the counter said. She held up Gobi's pet passport. "It's all in Chinese. If I can't read it, I can't let you on."

Not again, Dion thought! Then he remembered. Kiki had given him a pile of papers for when they reached Britain. "Will these work?" he asked, digging the papers out of his bag. They had all the same information as Gobi's pet passport, but in English.

The clerks looked everything over, and finally nodded. "Yes, you're good to go," they said. They stamped Gobi's passport and waved the three of them on board.

Getting into Britain turned out to be the easy part. They got off the ferry, then drove to Edinburgh. All of

Dion and Lucja's friends and family were waiting inside their home, eager to welcome them back and to finally meet Gobi in person.

Gobi also got to meet her sister Lara, a ragdoll cat, for the first time, and began to make friends with this new strange-looking animal.

It was a wonderful time, and Dion was thrilled to see everyone. Gobi loved the attention, too, but all three of them breathed a sigh of relief when everyone else finally left. Now it was just them, the way it should be.

And Dion knew just how to really welcome Gobi to Edinburgh, and how to prove to her that this was her new home, here with them.

"Come on, Gobi," he said, looking down at her with a huge grin on his face. "Let's go for a run."

The End